Is It
Friday
Already?

Dennis Ostapyk

Is It Friday Already?
© Copyright 2003 by Dennis Ostapyk
All rights reserved

International Standard Book Number:
1-894928-32-6

Printed in the United States of America

Dedication

This book is dedicated to my pet hamster, Joey. It was Joey's unrelenting drive and determination and total lack of wisdom that provided me the wherewithal to undertake this huge project of recording my diatribes for posterity's and Pete's sakes.

Witnessing the little vermin spend hour after hour, day after day, running in his wheel, expensing all his time and energy to get absolutely nowhere, caused me to deeply ponder my own status in life. I finally determined that we had a lot in common, little Joey and I.

Joey remained in exceptional health, so I thought, throughout his brief life. All of his efforts in his little wheel allowed him to remain quite trim and fit, until that fateful day when he suffered a massive heart attack and his little wheel slowly squeaked to a halt.

So Joe, I dedicate this book to you knowing full well that you couldn't care less. But hopefully for others who may also be spinning their wheels in life's many quagmires, this book may provide a smile, a respite in their journeys.

Forward

Have you ever found yourself on an airplane sitting beside someone who just won't shut up? That's where I found myself recently. To politely excuse myself I said to my neighbor, "I have some work to do," and reached into my bag to pull out Dennis' manuscript.

As I sat there reading while flying over the prairies below, I found myself laughing out loud, then quickly excusing myself as the people sitting near by stared at me quizzically.

I have had the pleasure of working with Dennis for several years and I have always found his writing to be extremely funny and creative. He has a way of finding and communicating the humor in life's daily activities. I think that one of the reasons his material has become so popular is because we can all relate to Dennis' subject matter. In fact, recently one of the stories from this book was published in a major newspaper.

Humor in the workplace has an amazing effect on the overall environment. I have seen our staff scurry to their computers on Friday mornings just to read Dennis' latest creation.

As you laugh your way through this book, please remember to share these stories with fellow employees, friends and family. "Is It Friday Already?" will turn the doldrums of your day into a moment of hilarious light!

Jeremy Braun
President
Word Alive Inc.

Introduction

Let me begin by stating outright that I did not want to write this book. Many people forced me into writing it. It was a conspiracy of sorts. I can't possibly, and therefore won't, mention all those involved in the enticement, because I haven't as yet forgiven them for prodding me into undertaking this huge endeavor.

Don't get me wrong, I love to write. I always have. I constantly looked forward to, and thoroughly enjoyed, turning my computer on at work every morning, Monday to Friday, and composing a little story about any topic that happened to pop into my head. A tidbit from the newspaper, from the radio or television, from a grade eight history class, an adventure with a family member, something overheard while eavesdropping, or dissecting a Children's Bedtime Story or Nursery Rhyme so as to uncover the *true* meaning and moral versus the one implied.

I received much adulation over the years from my peers for my writings. I greatly appreciated this. I soon discovered that my "**Morning E-Mails**", as they became to be known, were being forwarded by some of the staff members to their friends and family throughout the city and its environs, as well as out of province.

The many accolades and notes of appreciation that I was receiving however, slowly over time, took on the guise of an expectant demand for my creative thought processes. If I happened to miss sending out a **"Morning E-Mail"**, I would be thoroughly reprimanded and chastised by a few of the more demonstrative staff. I actually received the odd threat when I would neglect sending out a story for several consecutive days. I dismissed these threats as being inconsequential as they were relatively minor in nature. For example, I was threatened with having my lunch stolen from the refrigerator in the staffroom and eaten; of having my comb or calculator ribbon stolen, or my coffee cup defaced.

The most serious threat that I received was when I announced that I would be leaving on a two-week vacation at the end of that month. An anonymous note was slipped under my office door that morning demanding that I pre-write enough stories so that they could be e-mailed to the staff on each of the mornings that I was absent. The **"OR ELSE"** part of the note said something to the effect that I "would not be able to recognize my office upon my return". Also, my assistant threatened to quit while I was away if I didn't concede to the demands in the note from her co-conspirator.

So I stayed late a few evenings at the office

to compose these ten new stories. I didn't really mind much, because as I stated earlier, I love to write. What did concern me to some degree however, was the final comment on the bottom of the clandestine note, **"AND THEY'D BETTER BE GOOD!"**

As so often happens in most businesses, staff come and staff go. Upon saying good-bye to many of those who were leaving our employ from time to time, I was strongly urged to forward my **"Morning E-Mails"** to them at home or to their new places of business. I stated to them that this would not be ethical, and that I didn't feel like doing it anyway. It was during one of these confrontations that the notion arose among the staff that I should produce a book that would contain several of my "better" stories. This idea gained such momentum that no matter what I did I could not de-rail it.

So here is my book and here are my stories.

*Note of apology

I will apologize at the outset to any female readers who may be offended by any sexist remarks that are contained in this book.

Having said this, I will also remind you that I am a male, which automatically makes me right more than fifty-percent of the time.

A Formal Declaration

Dear Ladies,

Never, never, never take a male with you when you are shopping for a dress, **especially** if it is for a formal gown, and **especially** if the male happens to be your husband.

When our eldest son's wedding date was set, my wife decided that she needed to purchase a gown for the occasion. Fine. She also decided that I should go along with her to give my "opinion" in helping her to pick out "just the right one". Not fine.

This at first innocuous experience, took on epic proportions as the initially anticipated outing, slowly evolved into a grueling three-week ordeal. Every weekend, plus the odd week-night for three consecutive weeks, I was dragged around to every store in the city that sells these expensive one-night wonders. The decision to purchase our present house was made with less consideration, less deliberation, less shopping around, and in far less time. But then, of course, you don't have to **wear** a house in public. You can always **change the colour** of a house to match your shoes. You don't much care if there is **another house just like yours** on the planet, and you don't **use a house only once** and then abandon it to be forgotten about forever, unless you're Richard Gere.

After about the fiftieth hour everything starts to look good to the man. "Oh, look at this lime and mauve number over here! And you have a pair of silver shoes that will go just perfectly with it!" " What about that red one over there with the wolverine collar? That will never go out of style! It's a classic!" " I know this one looks like a tent, but I can always wear my khakis instead of a tuxedo so that we will compliment each other."

I overheard a youngster of about three years of age (male, of course), say to his mother in one of these stores, "Mommy, I don't want to be here!"

In yet another store, a four-year-old (another male, of course) was a little more succinct. "This place sucks!" he bemoaned, as he rolled around on the carpeted floor holding his stomach as if he were suffering physically from a malady induced by maternally forced boredom.

Surprisingly few of the many dress shops that we ventured into contained any sort of furniture for fatigued males to rest upon while the women flitted about in glorious bliss. I mean, are men **not expected** to be found in such establishments? Or are we expected to endure mental **and** physical suffering throughout? Several times I found myself catching a minute's rest for my weary legs by sitting on window ledges, stairways, on furniture in display showcases with other dummies, even on the floor in inconspicuous areas like behind racks of merchandise that **_wasn't_** on sale, or when really desperate, I would sneak into an unoccupied fitting room in order to plant my butt in a chair for a minute or two before being kicked out by some huffy salesclerk.

A washroom for men? Fie! (Shakespearean for "Ha!")

Towards the last days of this trial I began taking medication before venturing out to once more join the melee of female procrastinators.

My "opinions" by the way, the main purpose for which I was brought along, were completely ignored from the outset. Apparently my opinions on style, length, colour, price, etc. of apparel, would have served a loftier purpose for an Amazonian tribe's celebration of the "killing of the monkey" than for our son's wedding.

So please ladies, if we go dress shopping with you, it's only a gesture to be nice; or to put it another way...a carnal act of survival. It really is purgatory for us and we hate it right from the time that we're old enough to know better, which if I can use the two little boys I spoke of earlier as a measuring stick, would be somewhere around the age of two and a half years old.

By the way, other than those two little guys, I was keenly aware of a conspicuous inconspicuousness of other males in these stores, which leads me to two possible conclusions:

1. I am not as secure in my marriage as the males who were fearless enough to say, "No" to dress shopping, and stayed at home to watch hockey, or (and most likely)
2. These other males **were** actually present in these stores but were just not visible unless one happened to check the stairwells or change rooms, or stared at a dummy in a showcase window long enough to see if those glazed eyes would occasionally blink or not!

The Running of the Bears

There is a huge event that takes place annually in the town of Paloma, Spain. It is called the "running of the bulls".

In case you've never heard of this event, what happens is that a group of cabaleros who possess much exuberance and little sense, round up a herd of the meanest, ugliest bulls in Spain and stampede them through the narrow streets of Paloma. The real fun begins when men, for a variety of reasons only they could possibly know, jump out in front of this thundering herd and begin to run like the dickens in an attempt to stay ahead and not get trampled to death.

Local residents as well as spectators from around the world converge on this tiny town to cheer these brave men on. They witness the event from the rooftops of houses and buildings and from every window that overlooks the streets involved.

If you are one of the participants in this event, and you happen to trip and fall, you are trampled first by the other maniacal men following behind you, and then by the bulls. If you are too slow afoot, you get gored by the bulls and tossed several meters skyward and probably die.

The success of the event is measured by how many of the participants don't die.

Although women rarely participate in this adventure, as they fail to see the fun in it, an elderly woman was seriously injured last year when she approached a crosswalk in the centre of town, extended her arm to cross the street, and proceeded to walk straight into the path of the thundering, crazed mass of men and beef.

Anyone and everyone is eligible to participate as a contestant, the only criteria being a demonstrative absence of lucidity and/or a strong taste for tequila. The most successful participants usually possess a large degree of both.

But actually Spain isn't the only country that can boast such an exciting and fun filled event. In Bearclaw, Manitoba, which is approximately two hundred and thirty-seven and one quarter miles due north of Flin Flon, they host a similar event annually. They call it "the running of the bears".

A bunch of polar bears is first captured and then released on the outskirts of the town. An attempt is then made to drive these bears through the town's only street with fleeting Eskimos and other athletic natives running before them.

The town's population has been in decline

ever since the inception of these games. From one hundred and thirty-five inhabitants in 1979, when the run first began, it has dwindled to the current population of eighty-nine. The main problem it seems, is the official's inability to stampede the bears. Sneaking up behind them and yelling "hoy, hoy" while prodding them with sharp sticks, does little more than agitate the one ton creatures to the point of turning on the officials.

The few bears that do not get a piece of the officials and are still hungry, usually then stroll down the street helping themselves to any garbage, truck tires, or stray cats and dogs that may be around.

The contestants in "the run" continue to make the effort to be competitive by walking around town looking for a bear that may perhaps chase after them. Most don't usually get very far. Especially those wearing snowshoes.

If you ever get the notion to take this event in, it happens every year on January 28 in Bearclaw. The town is always looking for new contestants for this event and also for new inhabitants. The town offers major incentives to entice newcomers such as extremely high wages, political appointments with the purchase of a house, and free helicopter service to the Flin Flon hospital for all who participate in the "running of the bears".

Wright or Wrong

I'm quite sure that you all know that Wilber and Orville Wright, better known as "The Wright Brothers", spent many years of their lives studying, designing, building and testing their aviation invention.

But what I bet you didn't know was that their sole purpose for designing and building a contrivance that actually flew, was so that they could commit suicide.

It is not recorded in history, but Wilber and Orville hated their names so immensely that they could just not function in life with any degree of normalcy. Their father, Clyde Wright, and their mother Trixie, found a note left by the brothers on the morning of their inaugural flight, stating that if their flight was successful they would be dead by supper time. The note was not signed for obvious reasons.

We all know that their flight was very much a success, in our estimation, as they actually flew a distance of about three hundred feet. But the fifteen feet they gained in altitude was insufficient to accomplish their **real** goal.

Wilber did make his best effort to perform a nose-dive into the farm field at Kitty Hawk, but he could not bring "The Flyer" perpendicular to the ground. All that his best effort could produce was a minor somersault.

The two brothers did not take any solace in their fame that followed either, as the front page of the "Kitty Hawk Daily" illustrated a large picture of the two aviators including their entire family, with all of their names printed below in large, bold print;

Wilber and Orville	-the inventors
Clyde and Trixie	-the proud parents
Frodo	-brother
Shania-May-June	-sister
Murray	-dog

The Driver's Test

Next week I will be taking my sixteen-year-old son for his driver's test. I hope that he does better than I did when I took mine some thirty odd years ago. I failed at my first attempt, although it totally wasn't my fault.

Everything was going along fine until I came across an elderly gentleman riding his bicycle along a somewhat busy Winnipeg Street. Apparently, according to my tester, I passed the old guy too closely and then cut him off.

Personally, I don't think that I would have failed my test for doing just this if the old guy hadn't lost control of his bike and jumped the curb. If he was that unsure and unstable he shouldn't have been on the road in the first place.

Unfortunately for me there were several witnesses to this event leaving me no recourse. Actually, a number of these witnesses were also victims.

After the old gentleman cleared the curb he was totally out of control. He drove down the sidewalk a short distance wobbling side to side with legs flailing and feet running along the pavement trying to stop his erratic locomotion. He managed to elude a newspaper dispenser and streetlight standard as his countenance quickly changed from that of shock to terror.

When he rode into the crowd of people standing at a bus stop on the corner, it was surreal, like a dream unfolding in slow motion due to the fact that he was traveling at such a minor speed.

Then the commotion really began! Women began screaming while darting in every direction trying to get out of his path. Trying to dodge the meandering missile was very difficult to do, due to the way he was jerking the handlebars from side to side trying in vain to gain control.

Two men and a teenage girl made a brave attempt to get close to the reckless marauder in a combined effort to bring him to a halt. This proved to be fruitless however, as they could not gain proximity due to the many bodies scattered about like bowling pins in his wake.

The horrible episode finally came to an end when the panic-stricken cyclist broadsided a parked vehicle, which brought the bicycle to an abrupt halt. After a slight pause, the cycle tipped over sideways and fell to the ground with the old gent still in the saddle.

No one was injured during this fiasco, but there were some that were a little shaken up.

I had the notion to explain to my tester that this whole terrible incident was not my fault;

that Evil Knievel Sr. had no business being on the road if he couldn't control his vehicle. But I quickly dismissed this thought when I observed the look on my tester's face. I had witnessed this look once before many years ago. It was on my father's face when he discovered my brothers and I using his new parka as a net while playing street hockey.

Anyway, I will ensure that my son learns from my experience by instructing him of the possible danger of unruly cyclists that may be roaming the streets searching for an accident to get involved in!

Why Settle For Less?

Having lived most of my life on the Canadian prairies, I offer this short history lesson of what life on the prairies was like some five hundred years ago, or five hundred billion years ago if you happen to be a proponent of evolution.

Everyone knows that the Red River, which flows through the Dakotas and Manitoba, floods almost every year. Why the heck then, did the early settlers bother to settle here? And why were they forced to do battle with the Native Canadians, who first possessed this land, in order to **take it** from them?

In actual fact, the Natives **relinquished** this land **freely**. They had had enough with all the flooding, mosquitoes, and cold winters. Every spring it was the same old thing, "Ug, look Running Raccoon, river flood again. Me tired of soggy moccasin. I 'um out'a here!"

The tribe was then forced to pack up their teepees and head for the hills of Saskatchewan. But before they left, they named the area that they were vacating "Winnipeg", which means, "The Land of Flooding Waters, Horkin'-big Mosquitoes, and Friggin' Cold Winters".

They then wandered around Saskatchewan

for forty years looking for a hill, or manna, or actually **any** suitable place to live. Finally one of the scouts, Lumbering Ox, happened to stumble across a tremendous jawbone half buried in the earth. No one had ever seen such a large jawbone before, although warrior, Leaping Lizard, did comment that it sort of reminded him of his mother-in-law.

Since the largest animal that they had ever seen was a moose, they named the area "Moose Jaw", and settled there thinking that if the game was **this** large in this area, it would serve their best interests to hang around there for awhile.

Little did they know that the jawbone was actually that of a dinosaur. When this fact was finally discovered by the European settlers some two hundred years later, these new settlers wanted to change the name of the settlement to "Stygomorphiosauris Jaw". They later agreed however, that this name would not fit on the "**WELCOME TO**" sign on the outskirts of the settlement, so they decided that it would be too much of a hassle to make the change and therefore abandoned the idea.

Hence Moose Jaw kept its name even though there are no moose anywhere in the area. The Natives, however, **did** come across a great number of what they called,"lagunta" which literally translates,"Buffalo with shell of turtle". The European settlers later shortened this to"Pickup Truck".

I Love to Frown

It is a physiological fact that it takes fewer muscles in your face to smile and more muscles to frown.

This is precisely the reason why I try never to smile or laugh. The way I see it is that if I frown a lot, my face is exercising more! That is why my face is in such good shape for my age. I may be overweight in other areas of my anatomy, but at least my face is well toned. And let's face it (pun intended), your face is the most obvious and most important part of your body, no matter what most men may think to the contrary.

Actually, I try to scowl as often as I can. This is an extremely hard exercise to do, but it really burns off the calories and does wonders for the ol' kisser. I try to do at least twenty scowls a day. Your family and friends can really help you out with this exercise by getting on your nerves. I find that my kids are always willing to help out in this area.

Another little trick I've learned to help me with my scowling exercises is to undertake an almost impossible, unrewarding task that will frustrate the heck out of you, and leave you scowling for fifteen, or sometimes up to thirty minutes if you're lucky. Just last week I began a two thousand-piece jigsaw puzzle of Osama Bin Laden's cave and surrounding desert countryside. Or, if the opportunity presents itself to undertake **this** almost impossible, unrewarding task, try complimenting your mechanic.

A very good example of the point that I am trying to make is Santa Clause. Santa smiles and laughs way too much. He is just too darned jolly for his own good. That is why his face is so plump and he has to hide it with whiskers. He should really try frowning and scowling to tone up his facial features.

So don't jump to conclusions when you see someone with an angry look on his or her face, they may just be exercising it. And for your own sake, try not to look so happy all the time! Make the effort to look grumpy more often. You may lose some friends, but hey, think about how great you'll look when you're eighty!

-Have a great day! (just don't show it!)

So You're Growing Old, Eh!

Some of the figures in the Bible lived very long lives, like three hundred to nine hundred years. They must have had hundreds of children, grandchildren, great-grandchildren, great-great grandchildren, and great-great-great grandchildren. Can you imagine their family gatherings? They'd have to kill a flock of sheep in order to have the family over for a barbecue.

There would be births, weddings and funerals every day of the year.

"Noah dear, Ham* is turning one hundred next Friday. We should really do something for him."

"OK dear, you start sending the invitations and I'll start killing sheep."

And what do you give your wife on your four hundred and fiftieth wedding anniversary that she doesn't already have? I mean, how many clay pots does a woman need?

Do the kids live at home until they're two hundred and fifty?

How many diapers would a six hundred-year-old mother of eighty have changed in her lifetime?

Planning a camping trip would take years of advance preparation, and the trip would probably resemble the Israelites' departure from Egypt.

Do you ever hear such things as, "Don't eat that fat on the lamb chops! You'll have a heart attack by the time you're three hundred!" or, "Boy, where have the years gone! It seems like only yesterday that that glacier passed through here!"

Did they ever get bored? "So Isaac, what are you going to do today?"

"Well Dad, I think that I'll tend some sheep, maybe have some fruit for lunch, hang out at the oasis for awhile, have some mutton for dinner, and then play my harp for the rest of the evening. More or less the same thing that I've done every day for the past two hundred and eighty years."

And how about the little tike who wanted a pet dog for his very own?

"OK Jessie, if you can manage to behave yourself and be a very good boy for the next seven years, you can have a dog."

Noah's family must have been ecstatic when told by God to build an arc...

"We get to build an aaaaarrrrc! We get to build an aaaaarrrrrc!"

It mattered little that they were in the middle of a desert. They now had a project, something that they never would have dreamt of themselves, to occupy them.

What would be classified as middle age? Three hundred?

At what point would Noah hear the following from his wife:

"I'm starting to look so old! Look at all this gray hair! And these wrinkles! I sure can't move around the way I used to when I was five hundred and seventy-five!"

"You look fine dear. Let's have another kid. That always cheers you up!"

Deaths must have been very difficult to bear after knowing the person for centuries."He was so young. Only three hundred and five. He had his whole life ahead of him!" or, "How am I and my sixty-one sons and fifty-two daughters ever going to manage without our Ezekiel! Who's going to kill all the sheep around here now?"

All I can say is that it is a very good thing that the tradition of birthday cakes with candles did not appear for many, many years afterwards! Or just maybe... that was what the "pyre of flame" was. Maybe it was actually Moses's birthday!

*I always wondered why a Jewish family would name their son 'Ham'.

Don't Stop to
Smell the Roses!

One beautiful, sunny, Saturday, April afternoon, my lovely wife dragged me out to the "Greenhouses of St. Mary's Road" to enjoy the experience of helping her shop for plants and flowers for our yard.

If there are any young guys out there who have not had the opportunity to partake in this annual adventure, please take the word of a seasoned veteran and **don't do it!** I pray that you will learn from my experience.

As we entered the front doors I was almost knocked off my feet. The 'odoriferousness' that I encountered was incredible! I had never before been in a hot, humid, confined area with a hundred women before. The combined effect of such a vast variety of perfumes and hairsprays was overpowering!

Most of these women were there for the day! I could tell this because many of them were carrying lunch bags and wearing sneakers. They were not in any hurry, but pushed their carts down the long, narrow aisles at a snail's pace, thwarting any efforts for others to pass. They would then stop in the middle of the aisle pondering the purchase of a zenthanthrumum while a long line of shoppers built up behind them.

Now, this is the extent of my knowledge of foliage: if it is long and green, it is grass; if it is green and thicker than grass it is a bush; if it is green and tall, it is a tree; and if it smells and has colour, it is a flower.

As we ventured in a bit further I asked my wife, "Do we need a cart?"

"No, I just need to pick up a few things," was her reply.

Shortly thereafter, with a bag of sheep manure tucked under one arm, while trying at the same time to somehow balance four potted plants of various sizes, I made the decision to stumble back to the front of the store to procure a cart.

Upon my return, my wife caught my gaze with doe eyes as she held up a twenty pound fuchsia plant with a smile that could melt a polar ice cap. When I spotted the price tag dangling from the pot I quickly attempted to dissuade the purchase. I frantically began to rattle off a litany of excuses as to why we did not need, and should not spend that kind of money for, a plant the name of which I didn't even know how to spell, and that would be dead in a couple of months.

It was at this point that I began to feel faint. I don't really know if it was the heat and the humidity inside the greenhouse, or the overpowering vapors of perfume and hairspray, or the anticipated panic when our purchases were totaled up.

Finally at the checkout, our cart over-loaded with all kinds of vines, and grasses, and flowers, and other biological stuff to ensure that they would not all be dead by Monday, my wife wandered away to talk to a stranger about all the bunnies he had visiting his yard, leaving me alone with the cart full of stuff in the checkout line. The line was moving slower than a snail with a hernia. Directly behind me were two women that I could overhear talking. One of them said to the other, "My, doesn't he have a beautiful perineseum!" I was just about to turn around to thank her for the compliment when I realized that she was talking about something that was in my cart. One of the women then asked me what size pot I had. I replied, "thirty-six inches", somewhat surprised at this odd and personal question directed at me from a perfect stranger. They smiled and responded, "Your fuchsia, is it a fourteen or six-teen inch pot?"

When it was finally my turn to be checked out, the cashier began firing questions at me about whether these green and coloured things were perennials, centennials, or birenni-als, and how many dipthyriums I had in my cart. I began to panic and to perspire. I swiveled my head around in an effort to locate my wife. As she was too engrossed in conver-sation, and too far away for me to yell to her, I turned back to the clerk, wiped the perspiration from my brow, and told her to take her best guess.

Her parting words to me were to make sure that my rearendum got lots of sun. I assured her that it would, and left skid marks as I pushed my cart out the front door.

I left the "Greenhouses of St. Mary's Road" a broke and embarrassed man, which was a small price to pay considering the enormous beauty all of the green and coloured things provided our yard that summer!

History 101

How well do you know your American History? I think that most of us are aware that July 4 is the date celebrated as America's Independence from England, when the United States became a nation. But what else do you remember from your history classes concerning this monumental event? Let me refresh your memory.

On July 4,1776 a bunch of Independent Fathers got together and had a tea party. Among those present were George Washington, the man with the mahogany smile, (he had wooden teeth), John Handcock who later became famous for his sprawling signature, and Benedict Arnold who later was tried as a traitor for smuggling Colombian coffee into the tea party. Benjamin Franklin was supposed to be there but showed up late. He made a spectacle of himself so the other Fathers told him to go fly a kite.

While at the tea party the Independent Fathers got to talking, and decided that it would be a good idea to put something famous down in writing, so that they would all have a solid alibi to give to their respective wives as to why they were spending so much time together drinking tea. So they began...

All men are created equal. Period.

All women are **not** equal to men...

they cannot vote

they cannot work outside the home

they cannot hold public office

they cannot demonstrate or present their opinions in a public forum

they cannot be ministers, pastors, or elders in a church

they cannot drink or smoke or enter certain establishments frequented by men

they cannot compete in the Olympics

they cannot question their husbands

they cannot question tea parties

they cannot grow old or become over-weight

they cannot have headaches past 8:00 P.M.

Now this was only the first article! This document went on to cover all areas relevant to the times as they were in 1776.

The women were furious when they caught wind of what the Fathers were up to! (The Fathers never found out who leaked the contents of their discussions before they were completed, but many suspected Benedict Arnold. A few of the Fathers actually went out and egged his house one night, hence the name "Eggs Benedict" came about).

Anyway, the most important article, which has since been amended sixty-two times and now bears absolutely no semblance at all to what was originally intended, went something like this...

"We, being of sound mind and full of tea, do hereby proclaim that we are truly independent. We can go wherever and do whatever we please. No woman can tell us what to do. We can spend time with our kids, or not. It is entirely up to us. If George here, for example, wants to cut down the cherry tree in his front yard, he can do so. Martha has no say in the matter".

Now this was the law of the land for many decades until the suffragettes came along and suffocated the article and caused it to be amended.

So now you know why Americans celebrate July 4. The men get together and drink tea and talk about "the good old days" when they were truly independent, before the suffragettes came along and ruined everything. They then eat chicken and pie that their wives have prepared, and then of course, there are the fireworks later on when they retire with their wives for the night.

For the Birds

Where does the saying, "He or she eats like a bird" come from anyway? It **can't** mean that he or she doesn't eat much, based on the beasts that frequent our backyard!

My wife has eighteen (18) birdfeeders scattered about our backyard that attract anything from sparrows to hummingbirds to woodpeckers to storks, to chickadees, to ducks and geese, to escaped budgie birds, etc., etc., etc. She has to refill these feeders twice daily; first thing in the morning, and upon arriving home from work around six o'clock in the evening. And these are **huge** feeders, each containing about eight pounds of various types of seed

Needless to say, there is a considerable amount of "pigging out" happening in our backyard. Most all the birds that are regular diners have become obese. I have witnessed six-pound sparrows failing at getting airborne because their tiny wings could not lift their blimp-like bodies off the ground.

One day from our kitchen window I saw a group of several plump sparrows waddle across our yard and congregate under a feeder that was hanging from a tree branch. The lead bird, wearing spiked boots, lumbered up the trunk of the tree and then shuffled along a branch until its weight caused the branch to bow to the ground allowing the others to climb aboard the feeder for their rather lengthy repast.

Many migratory birds that have lost their ability to gain flight now spend their winters in our backyard. The long, cold winters of Manitoba eventually begin to gnaw at these feathered footballs, with the result that most develop "an attitude" by mid-February.

Oftentimes we have been disturbed by a banging on our backdoor by a hefty robin demanding worms. Juncos dive-bomb my family and I en masse when they want the birdbath water warmed up. A woodpecker once punted the suet we had left on our picnic table, illustrating his disgust at our seemingly lack of variety in menu planning.

It is a very sad, sorry and sordid sight.

So please be careful when using the analogy, "My, you eat like a bird!" because it may carry negative connotations which you could never have imagined!

Ranger: (witnessing two men cooking over an open fire)
"What are you cooking in that pot? Don't you know that there are no open fires allowed this time of year?"

Man: "This is whooping crane stew.

We're sorry, we didn't know about the ban on fires."

Ranger: "Forget the fire! Don't you know that the whooping crane is an endangered species? You can't go around killing these birds!"

Other man: "We're terribly sorry! We didn't realize it was a whooping crane until after we'd shot it."

Ranger: "Well, OK. I won't fine you this time, but be more careful in the future!
By the way, what does whooping crane taste like anyway?"

Man: "Uhhh, somewhere between bald-headed eagle and stork.

Don't Forget to Bring Your Harmonica

Speaking of harps, will all of us (most of us, some of us, I) be playing harps when we get to heaven? Where does it specifically say in the Bible that angels will fly around playing harps? Could it be because thousands of years ago there were only three types of musical instruments and they had to make a choice between the harp, the lyre or the drum? Can I play my guitar when I get there? Or is it just the harp or nothing? Some ethereal flute music would be nice. I hope bagpipes remain here on earth and that the saxophone remains in New Orleans where it belongs. And while I'm at it, I bet I know where rap is going! That's reason enough to stay on the straight and narrow right there!

I sincerely apologize to all the bagpipe, saxophone, rapper, jazz lovers out there. I am asking for forgiveness because I want to be up there one day playing my harp (or guitar). I can't even contemplate eternal rap!

You didn't know that I played guitar? Yes, I

am a musician, singer-songwriter in my spare time when I am not playing at being an accountant. My friend and partner, Bob, and I form the duo, **"Those 2 Guys"**.

One evening **"Those 2 Guys"** were performing at a local restaurant/coffee house. We were in the middle of our second set of the evening and had just completed a song, when some guy in the audience stood up and yelled, "What do you do with a drunkin' sailor?"

How was I supposed to know that he was requesting a song? Most patrons write their requests on a napkin and bring it up to us. I thought that this guy was heckling us so I answered back, "I don't know, but you're about to find out!" I then promptly asked one of the waitresses to call the cops to have the bum thrown out.

For some reason this guy took offense to this. As he made his way toward the stage with his half-eaten torte in his hand, his foot caught on the leg of a chair causing him to stumble and fall, planting his face into his torte and then into the floor. This embarrassment in front of a full house of spectators caused him to become even further agitated. He scraped the torte from his face and wound up to throw it at me, but the torte slipped out of his hand on his backswing and ended up in his girlfriend's hair. As she jumped up in surprise, her knees banged the table she was seated at causing it to flip over, dumping its contents onto the patrons who were seated at the table next to them.

This caused even further commotion, which allowed me time to arm myself. I stood up and grabbed my guitar by its neck to use as a shield against any other missiles that might be thrown, or as a club in case he made any further attempts to get close to me.

The situation didn't progress that far however, as his now 'ex-girlfriend', poured her cup of hot mocha latte down the back of his collar. Two younger fellows then intercepted him and showed him to the parking lot.

He ended up getting his just desserts, so to speak. I didn't like the looks of him right from the minute that he walked into the café. He had the air of a bagpipe lover!

Reichter

Hans Reichter was a German physicist who lived between 1887-1965. He is credited with developing "The Reichter Scale" which measures earth tremors and earthquake severity.

What you may **not** know about Reichter, is that his invention was discovered quite by accident. He was **actually** conscripted by the German Government to study the effects of bratwurst and sauerkraut on the German people and on the environment.

Due to the highly volatile effects of bratwurst and sauerkraut, (especially when ingested with German Beer and Polkas), the studies of Reichter were quite dangerous and clandestine. (For those who have ever attended Octoberfest, they can attest to this, I'm sure)

It was in the midst of these studies and experimentation that Reichter realized that his new invention was **not** picking up the percussions from the corner pub on Friday night, but was actually recording earth tremors from a thousand miles away.

Although he never solved the country's bratwust-saurkraut problem, Reichter became a famous name in history on the offshoot invention "The Reichter Scale".

Burnt Offering

I love to cook and bake, although I don't do it very often. I have come to a conclusion as to why men don't cook or bake as often as they would actually like to.

Firstly, if they are married, their wives most probably hide or disguise the stuff that they need so that they can't find it. I don't know if this is done purposefully or not.

Example:

I decided one day to bake a cake from scratch (not from a box of mix). The recipe called for baking powder. I opened the cupboard where I suspected the baking powder might be located, and staring me in the face were five plastic bags of white stuff. (My wife buys in bulk)

Now as she was not at home to ask, and I wanted the cake to be a surprise anyway, I had to surmise this conundrum on my own. I tried smelling the contents of each bag. No help, they were odorless. I tried tasting the contents of each bag. No help, who knows what baking powder tastes like anyway? I only eliminated the icing sugar using this technique. So I was now left with **four** bags of white stuff and I knew that one of them contained the baking powder that I needed. I also knew that one contained cornstarch, another contained baking soda, and the last I couldn't even guess. It may have been heroin. So I guessed, and guessed wrong. I used the cornstarch. My cake was flat and tasted like insulation. I sure did impress my family with my efforts though! And the Canada geese loved the cake!

Secondly, all cookbooks are sexist. I cannot understand the directions. They are written in some sort of universal language only known to women.

Example:

Directions in book for women	How men understand it
Beat	Mix it
Stir	Mix it
Blend	Mix it
Cream	Mix it
Mix	Mix it
Fold	Mix it
Add	Dump in
Pour	Dump in

Drizzle	Pour over
Sprinkle	Pour over
Let stand	Go for a smoke
Ingredients	Stuff
Preheat oven	Turn oven on at beginning of hockey game
Place cake in oven when at 350 degrees	Shove cake in oven at fifth commercial break
Remove when toothpick inserted comes out clean	Take cake out at first intermission
Allow to cool	Grab a hunk just before second period starts

Now barbecuing is a different story altogether. Traditionally, men do most of the outdoor cooking. No one really knows why. Maybe it's because they can drop food all around and just poke it through the spaces in the deck with their cooking tongs not having to worry about picking it up. They can break things, create clouds of smoke, drink beer at the same time, while no one really seems much to care.

Here is a series of steps that usually takes place at a barbecue:

1. Man fires up barbecue while woman prepares meat
2. Man puts meat on barbecue while woman prepares vegetables
3. Man sits and drinks beer while woman sets table
4. Woman comes out to tell man the meat is burning
5. Man serves the meat while the woman serves the salad, vegetables, beverages,dessert and coffee
6. Man puts away barbecue and talks to neighbour while woman does dishes
7. Man asks woman how she enjoyed his barbecue
8. Man experiences chill from woman's visage
9. Man surmises that "there is just no pleasing women"
10. Woman is **very** tired and develops a headache at bedtime.

If the Shoe Fits

Did you know that this year is the 275th anniversary of cement? Prior to 1728 construction materials consisted of stones, wood, or bricks held together with mud.

Around this time in Sicily, the beginnings of the Mafia were becoming evident. Many of the leaders, (Dons) were trying to come up with a better way of disposing of bodies after "elimination".

Digging shallow graves in the woods was too much work and too dirty a job. Leaving a freshly eliminated corpse propped up in a seat on a city bus or in a movie theatre was too risky. (Although, this particular method of disposal *was* quite successful when employed at cricket matches where a corpse could actually fit in with a crowd of cricket spectators for several days before being detected). Using rope to tie bodies to weights and then dumping them into the river was also proving not to be a very dependable method of disposal. The rope would eventually decay or slip off the weight, be eaten through by fish, or get caught up in boats passing over head allowing the body to float up to the surface.

The Sicilian craftsmen working for the Mafia, worked long and hard until they finally came up with a compound that was easy to mix and form into any shape. It was extremely heavy and would never wear away.

It was called '**cement**'.

The story goes that the first time this word was used...On his way to church one Sunday morning, Don Guesseppi Lavardi uttered the words, "**See**, I **meant** what I said" to his victim just before eliminating him. What he meant by this statement was that if Luigi Toppazzini didn't keep his nose clean, he would end up in the river feeding the fish. So the phrase "**See**, I **meant** it"came in vogue to mean to "ce-ment the deal".

From that day on, bodies were fitted with cement overshoes to take them to the depths of the river that runs through Sicily. In fact, this became such a popular practice that the river actually rose two feet in one year due to all the cement and bodies being dumped in.

And this is why even to this day Italians are the best at doing cement work. This art has been passed down through many eliminations.

It's a Pleasure to Meet You.
How Old Did You Say You Were?

While reading the newspaper this past weekend I noticed that in every article I read having to do with everyday current events involving people, other than politicians and the like, the ages of the individuals was always given.

I wonder why this is?

Examples:

"On Friday night two armed gunmen were involved in a home invasion at 136 Maple St., the home of Elton Feeber (47) and his wife Amber (19)."

"There was a fire last night in the downtown area at 2099 Main St. The estimated damage stands at $500,000. The lone occupant, Chester Rankman (62), was taken to hospital suffering from smoke inhalation and bad breath."

It's a Pleasure to Meet You.
How Old Did You Say You Were?

Just how important is it to know the ages of the individuals? Do reporters run up to the stretcher as it is being loaded into the back of an ambulance shouting, "Sir, Sir, how old are you Sir? Can you show me with your fingers if you're in too much pain to speak?"

When speaking to police after an accident do reporters say, "Oh, so he didn't make it. That's too bad. Did he happen to mention how old he was before he croaked?"

When reporting news about women, how would you ever know you're getting the truth anyway?

Policeman:	"Ah M'am, is that your cat stuck up in that tree? How old are you?"
Woman:	"Yes, that's my cat. 39."
Policeman (aside):	"Yeh right! She's old enough to be me grandmudder!"

The article – as it appears in the newspaper:
"Senior citizen's cat gets stuck in oak tree. Fire Department called to the rescue. Mrs. Olga Nostril (39) was frantic yesterday afternoon and dialed 911 when she couldn't find her pussy. She combed the entire neighbourhood in her wheelchair before..."

Next event...

"The suspected killer who robbed the bank and then jay-walked to his getaway car in broad daylight yesterday afternoon, was finally apprehended last night. Moose Nesterenko (32) of no fixed address, was taken into custody at a Tim Horton's. Not realizing his faux pas in that grabbing a bite to eat in a donut shop immediately following the crime when half of the patrons were cops, Moose surrendered peacefully after a brief struggle with one of the officers over the last walnut crunch."

Is this more or less how this arrest actually played out...?

"OK Moose, drop that walnut crunch, ***NOW!*** How old are you, ***TODAY!***"

Next event...

"Sir, did you witness this accident? Can I please get your name and your age?"

Really, what has age got to do with reporting the story? Why not include eye colour? Neck size? What he/she had for breakfast?

Newspaper Story:
"The only witness to the accident, Mr. Chuck Wagon, (51) (blue eyes) (size 16 neck) (pancakes for breakfast), says that he has never seen anything like it! Mr. Wagon reported that "all of a sudden the car just jumped

the curb, drove across the front lawn and through the front door of the house that the woman driver (46) (green eyes) (size 35 bust) (eggo's for breakfast), was headed for to visit a friend (44) (brown eyes) (size 50 pants) (McDonald's menu for breakfast). The driver's friend was somewhat startled when she ran to the front door of her house and saw the car halfway inside at which point she exclaimed, "How come you're so late?"

The Sisters of Destruction

Were you aware of a crack tactical unit that has been training in Quebec for years to counter any terrorism directed towards Canada? This has been a top-secret operation for over ten years which the media has just recently gotten hold of.

The unit consists of thirty commando-nuns, trained to infiltrate and annihilate the deadliest, most diabolical enemies. The "Sisters of Destruction" maintain a "take no prisoners" mandate. Most of the Nuns are between the ages of forty-five and sixty-five. At this age they exhibit the most nastiness and are extremely crotchety, but are still wiry enough to get the job done.

Armed with black leather straps and razor-sharp yardsticks, these Nuns can strike with such stealth that the enemy has no time to react before they are completely overcome by their swarming tactics.

The leader of the squad, Sergeant-Major Sister Mary Voracious, is the juggernaut of the group having over forty years of active duty and many successful missions.

I don't know about you, but I feel a whole lot better knowing that these commandos are protecting the safety of our country!

Disney Diatribe

Did you know that Walt Disney was terrified of mice and absolutely hated the little critters?

Early in his career, Walt was an amateur artist. One day he was sitting at his drawing table at home trying to come up with a special character that would have the potential of being developed into a unique cartoon feature hero. He was actually working on a duck at this instant in time named Donald. As he sat there drawing, a mouse came out from under a baseboard and scurried across the room and under Walt's chair.

Well, let me tell you, this just scared the beejeebers out of Walt!

Standing atop his chair with wet trousers and heart racing, he swore that he would get even with that little gray rodent some day.

All of a sudden Walt got a brain wave! He jumped back down into his chair and frantically began to draw, wet trousers and all.

He created a mouse and named him "Murray".

In his very first escapade, Walt creatively drew that Murray's tail got caught in a mousetrap. Yelling and screaming, Murray ran outdoors dragging the trap behind him. An owl that just happened to be flying over at the time spotted Murray and swooped down and picked him up and took Murray to its nest where it immediately plucked his eyes out.

Murray managed to escape the owl but because he could no longer see, he took a wrong turn while trying to get home and ended up at the waterfront. After staggering around for some time, Murray tripped over a rope and fell into a steamboat that shortly thereafter left the pier for the centre of the harbor.

Murray was famished! He managed to find some food, but just as he was about to dine he was thrown overboard with the garbage he was about to eat. A seagull happened to spot Murray and managed to rip one of his legs off before Murray could swim away to safety.

Murray managed to hobble home by following his nose, but just as he crossed the street in front of the house where he lived, he was run over by a steamroller and squashed. Even his mother wouldn't recognize him now!

Walt loved his new cartoon! He took it down to the studio the very next day. His colleagues thought the story stunk and that it was far too violent for a children's cartoon. They ended up changing "Murray" to "Mickey" and changed the whole story around so that Mickey was the captain of the steamboat.

"Steamboat Mickey" was the first cartoon ever produced. The rest is history.

So Mickey ended up making Walt very rich and famous, but Walt still hated his guts!

Let Us Give Thanks

Why do we celebrate Thanksgiving Day and when did it begin?

In the United States, Thanksgiving Day is on the fourth Thursday of November each year.

In 1618, William Penn, the mover and shaker Quaker who had the state of Pennsylvania named after him, went hunting for grouse to feed his starving family. Armed with his faithful blunderbuss that he affectionately named "Blunderbuss", he went tramping through the woods hoping to spot a grouse or even better, many greese. Suddenly he spotted some movement in a nearby bush. Without hesitation he aimed and fired. The spray of buckshot covered nine square meters. There was an immediate shower of feathers.

Approaching his kill he was delighted to see a huge bird lying there stone cold dead. It was enormous! It must have weighed at least thirty pounds.

"Boy, the greese sure are huge over here on this side of the ocean!"gleefully chuckled Bill as he dragged the bird home.

Bill and his wife, Melody, eviscerated the bird and stuffed it full of bread and fruit. They then crammed it into a cornucopia.

After the bird was cooked to perfection, the Penn family gave thanks to God for the abundance of food on their table and for the size of the greese in the colony.

This all happened on the fourth Thursday of November in 1618 as penned in Penn's diary.

As is usual with us Canadians, we eventually followed the Yanks, but it took much longer to solidify the holiday of Thanksgiving, which is on the second Monday of October. This date did not become an official holiday until 1923.

All Canadians up until this time were looking for something to be thankful for. But all they had encountered thus far was extremely cold winters, swarms of mosquitoes in the summer, wars, and Newfoundland.

Then it finally happened!

Finally something to be truly thankful for!

On the second Monday of October 1923, the first National Hockey League game was played in Ottawa.

The entire country took the day off to stay indoors and listen to the game on the radio, telecast by the CBC and Foster Hewitt. The very first sponsor for Hockey Night in Canada, was Tom's Turkey Ranch in Kemptville, Ontario, just outside of Ottawa.

Thus, this historical day was written into law as a National Holiday where the whole Nation of Canada could set aside the time to be truly thankful for hockey, and celebrate as a family with a huge turkey dinner while listening to the game.

Mime Your Own Business

If a mime fell in the forest,
Would he make a sound?

A mime was walking through the forest. He was hunting for a glass box. He was walking against the wind.

He suddenly found a glass box and climbed in. He thought that he was safe. But alas, he couldn't get out of the box.

The strong wind blew a tree over onto the box. The box got smashed to smithereens. The mime mimed a scream. No one heard him.

The tree crushed him to death. No one knew if he was really dead or just miming death.

He was placed in a glass coffin. All the mimes in the country pretended to go to the funeral. They mimed singing hymns and then all bowed their heads to observe twenty-one years of silence.

Just then the wind picked up so they all went for a walk against it.

(This has been a Mime-Time story)

Questions:

Do novice mimes first have to learn to walk against a breeze before they can walk against the wind? Can the veteran mimes walk in a hurricane? Why are they always out walking in bad weather anyway? Why don't they stay at home and play charades with their mime friends? Wouldn't that be something to see? One mime would be acting out a charade, let's say for example, "a glass box". The other mimes on his team would then be acting out their responses back to him. So then you would have the whole team acting out "a glass box". All the while the mimes on the opposing team would be miming amongst themselves, "I know this one! I know this one!"

I guess that it is quite obvious that I am not a great fan of miming. I did enjoy one once, however. He (or is it, It?) was being interviewed on the radio.

The Sports Page

Yes, I love watching sports, especially football. But do you know what I greatly dislike about watching football? It's the celebration dance that the players do in the end zone after scoring a touchdown. I get embarrassed everytime I witness this. It's not the actual dancing that embarrasses me, it's the fact that the white guys are never included in the celebration. We all know that the reason the white guys are not included, of course, is that they can't dance and would look idiotic trying to do so.

After a touchdown is scored, all of the black guys gather in the end zone and perform a choreographed routine while the white guys just leave the field, go to the bench, and high-five each other and get passed a water bottle. Ya gotta feel sorry for the poor white guys!

Can you imagine six white guys linking arms and trying to do some kind of choreographed "rap thing" in the end zone? The fans would most likely boo them, even if the game was being played on their home turf. It would probably be quite an ugly scene.

When a white guy scores a touchdown, usually the only move he can make to celebrate, is to spike the football. And some of them can't even do that right!

Take Kerwin Bell for example, former quarterback for the Toronto Argonauts. During a game being broadcast on National television, Kerwin became so excited after scoring a touchdown against his former team, the Blue Bombers, that he ran up to an opposing player and spiked the ball at his feet. The ball bounced off the hard artificial turf right back up into a vulnerable area of Kerwin. Kerwin was stunned by the blow and was knocked off balance. This caused him to then stumbled sideways and step on the back of the foot of another Bomber player. He was now totally off balance and went sprawling across the turf. You just gotta feel embarrassed for the guy! Especially since TNN replayed this several times during the game. They then chose this fiasco to be "the play of the game" and replayed it some more. It also made the highlight reel which was replayed the following week on all of the sports broadcasts.

So the next time that you watch a touchdown celebration dance in the end zone during a football game, remember the poor white guys on the bench saying to one another, "Gee, I sure wish I could do that! I wish that they would include me in their dance! I wish that I had an ounce of rhythm!"

And also think about poor old Kerwin Bell who was forced to retire from football because of bad judgment and a bad bounce.

Sports Page (continued)

One evening my son and I attended a baseball game here in town. We arrived at the ballpark quite early, and upon walking through the turnstile we were approached by a staff member of the home team. We were told that the person who was commissioned to throw out the ceremonial first pitch was ill and had to cancel out at the last minute.

This young man then asked me, "Are you anyone important?"

I answered, "No, but oftentimes I pretend to be."

He responded, "OK, I guess that will have to do! Would you like to throw out the first pitch tonight?"

I said, "Sure, why not!"

I was not the least bit intimidated as I possess an excellent throwing arm due to the significant amount of practice I get throwing projectiles at the many neighbourhood cats that frequent our yard.

Out on the mound awaiting the "go ahead", I decided to throw my three –fingered, forked spitball. This proved to be a bad decision! I must have used too much spit. Halfway through my delivery the ball slipped out of my grasp, and headed halfway between home plate and the home team's dugout.

The mascot should have been paying attention, but he wasn't. The ball bounced off his huge padded head, and careened into the dugout. The starting pitcher for the game tried to grab the stray ball with his bare hand before it could do any further damage, but committed an error in the dugout as the ball ricocheted off his right thumb and then bounced back onto the field.

This prompted even further commotion as it turned out that his thumb was broken! We later heard that he is done for the season.

They allowed my son and I to stay and watch the game but told me not to come back again until my suspension had been lifted.

If I wasn't anyone important when I walked into the ballpark, I surly was when I left!
What is the moral of this story?

a) When in doubt, go with the fastball.
b) Don't pretend to be someone who you're not.
c) Never rely on a mascot or a bumbling pitcher to get you out of a jam.

d) Don't go to baseball games.
e) A+B
f) B+A
g) C+D
h) D+A-B
i) (BxD-C)7y/3.14
j) All of the above.
k) Some of the above.
l) None of the above.
m) Who cares?

Toss Me Another Fig, Newton

One day Sir Isaac Newton was sitting under a tree reading a book. As he began to doze in the warm summer sun and gentle breeze, he was bopped on the head by an apple that fell from a branch up above. He was a little dazed at first, but after he regained his senses he asked himself the incredibly puzzling question, "Why did this apple fall down and not up?"

Now Sir Isaac, or Sir Izzy as he was affectionately known, had a <u>real</u> head on his shoulders. No one in recorded history had ever asked this question before. For thousands of years humankind had walked around on this earth having stuff fall on their heads like rain, fruit, arrows, catapulted rocks, pots, pans, and rolling pins from irate wives, and bird droppings, but had never wondered about this phenomenon or asked this totally baffling question. Izzy immediately ran home to tell his wife the good news.

"Honey", he gasped breathlessly, "did you know that objects fall down and not up? And if I throw something up into the air it will eventually fall back down and not continue to go up?"

Mrs. Newton stared at Izzy for a few seconds

in amazed silence. Then with tears welling up in her eyes she ran to her husband and threw her arms around him pleading, "Oh Izzy, please, can you ever forgive me for striking you so many times on the head with my pots and pans and rolling pin. I never realized that all those blows to your head would eventually turn you into a fruit cake!"

Now back in those days, of course, figs were very plentiful and cheap. (Do you see where I'm going with this?) So Mrs. Newton used this abundant supply of figs in the fruit-cakes that she baked on a regular basis. Thus, the name given today to pastries containing figs is "**Newtons**"and anyone who displays being a little "nutty" is called a fruitcake!

So if it weren't for **Mrs. Newton** and her rolling pin, not only would the immortal question, "Why do things fall down and not up" not have been answered by the understanding of gravity, but we also would not have any Fig Newton cookies to this very day! Believe it, or not! Or else!

Is It Only Me?

Please tell me that these kinds of things happen to everyone and not only to me! It will do wonders for my self-worth.

Why is it that whenever I am forced to make a visit to an ATM machine, that there is always a lineup for their use? And why are the people using them so slow? It's almost as if they **enjoy** doing their banking with one of these impersonal robotic computers. They must enjoy the thrill of punching **all** of the buttons and performing every transaction that is available. I seriously feel that some of them look upon these machines as slot machines, knowing that there is money in there somewhere and if they hit the right combination they'll hit the jackpot. I *always* find myself in a lineup at these things. And forget about seeing a teller! It would be easier to see the Pope!

Why is the first machine to become available to me always the wheelchair accessible one? I am six feet two inches tall! When I stand in front of this machine the screen would be the perfect height if my bellybutton were a third eye. I can't read the directions on the screen because of its angle in relation to my line of sight, and also due to the glare reflecting off of it from the overhead lights. I can't reach the keypad or put my papers and wallet on the tiny ledge without stooping over. I have found that the best thing to do in this situation is to get onto my knees. This is what I do most of the time. This way, everything works.

So while I'm waiting in line for fifteen minutes, just knowing that the three-foot tall monitor has my name on it, and it's **finally** my turn, so the next ATM is mine, sure enough, the customer using the wheelchair accessible machine turns and walks away. My knees immediately buckle as I receive confirmation that I'm headed for the munchkin machine. As I approach, my knees proceed to bend more and more until by the time I'm halfway to the machine I'm doing a Groucho Marx impersonation, and by the time I reach the machine, I am fully down on my knees and ready to conduct business.

Quite often I will then visit a Mal-Wart store which is in the vicinity. The greeter always recognizes me because of the dirty knees of my pants.

After I have picked up my single, solitary item, I head over to the cashiers. There are three of them. There are forty-six customers in each line. My line moves the slowest. All the other lines are moving faster than a hot knife through butter. Everyone in my line wants to pay by cash. They want to pay by **exact** cash. None of them has ever heard of legal tender. They empty their change purses and proceed to count out dimes, nickels, and pennies and then redeem all of the coupons that they've been saving since 1987. The cashier then re-counts everything just to make sure that her line doesn't move any faster than the ones on either side of her. But I really don't mind. It allows me some extra time to think about all the things that I could be doing if I wasn't standing in this lineup.

Finally I am only one person away from it being **my** turn. Nope, not yet! Hold everything! There is no bar code on one of the items the person ahead of me has selected. There are three million items on the store's shelves and this person had to pick up one with no bar code. Yes folks, it's price check city! I'm trapped! I can't escape! I begin to imagine the worst! I start to perspire! Will my debit card work, or am I at my limit? Does my single, solitary item have a bar code on it? Will I be able to purchase it before the store closes? Before the expiry date on my item is reached? Will the cashier close this line down before I can get through? Will I be able to get the dirt out of the knees of my pants?

Is It Only Me? (Part Two)

Well as it so happens, I was forced to visit Mal-Wart again the very next day. I didn't have to purchase anything, I was just there to get my son's watch repaired.

Upon entering, I exchanged greetings with the greeter, (she didn't recognize me because I hadn't been to the bank beforehand), and immediately noticed that there were sixteen cashiers on duty, and only six were attending customers. The other ten were standing out in the main isle chatting, while waiting for a stray customer to happen by to pounce upon.

"Why me?" I wailed to myself. " Why don't I have anything to purchase today? Why didn't I come shopping today instead of yesterday?"

While I was waiting around for the watch to be repaired, I wandered into the toy and games department and noticed a game on one of the shelves that I had never seen or heard of before. The name of the game was "Clawback". It appeared to be a very interesting game based upon the instructions that I read on the back of the box.

Any number of people can play, from two to infinity. A selected number of players form "The Government". It doesn't matter how many are in "The Government, as long as it's more than half of the total number of players. These selected players then don't do anything for the rest of the game. All of the play money is doled out equally among the other players. They then immediately must give one-half of their money to "The Government" no questions asked. They then must try to survive on what's left.

The players then roll the dice in sequence and move their pieces around the board paying for food, houses, clothes, children's expenses, transportation, entertainment, taxes, etc. trying not to go bankrupt before they die.

"The Government" continues to grow, clawing back one-half of everything that the players receive, no questions asked.

If a player should happen to go bankrupt, he is out of the game. He must then serve snacks and beverages to "The Government" for the rest of the evening. If a player happens to die during the course of the game, "The Government" takes over all of his possessions, and any additional indebtedness remaining to "The Government", is passed on to the player to the left of the deceased player.

After all the players are either bankrupt or dead, the game is over.

Wouldn't this be a great educational game for the kiddies to learn the realities of life?

There is a warning on the box stating that there is a strong possibility of fisticuffs breaking out during the playing of the game.

You can buy this game at Mal-Wart for $69.95, of which one-half is tax.

I Didn't Know That!

All of the following statements are 100% true:

Did you know...

- that most of us have swallowed a spider in our sleep?
(and that most married men have swallowed a giant hair ball in their sleep because their wives have forgotten to take their hair out of the buns on their heads before going to bed).

- that apples, not caffeine are more efficient at waking you up in the morning? (but most people still choose to use the alarm clock).

- that your feet are bigger in the afternoon than at any other time of the day? (that is why most place kickers suck in day games).

- that the average housefly lives for one month?

(but in that month each one mates 28,000 times and produces 83 million maggots).

- that babies are born without kneecaps? (they don't develop them until ages 2-6) (that is why they can crawl around on hardwood floors and bend themselves into the shape of a pretzel. It also explains why they are such excellent horsemen up to the age of six).

- that Alfred Hitchcock did not have a bellybutton?
  (but that was only on **one** of his stomachs).

- that forty people are sent to hospital every minute with dog bites?
  (I wish those forty people would leave the dogs alone!).

- that the toothbrush was invented in 1498?
  (but no one had teeth back then. It was actually first intended to be a hairbrush for midgets).

- that forty thousand Americans are injured by toilets each year?
  (and sixty thousand Canadians are injured by sinks? But the most vicious porcelain predator of all is, of course, the bathtub. The worst case in history thus far involved

a sixty-eight year old woman named Rose Foosmuth of Gary, Indiana. It appears that one morning Rose went into her bathroom with the intention of washing her face, using the john, and then taking a shower. She was never seen alive again. The police suspect that her death was gang related).

- that only 7% of the population is left-handed?
(and 93% of them are currently pitching in the major leagues).

- that if colouring weren't added to Coke it would be green?
(Pepsi would be yellow, Dr. Pepper would be pink, and Mountain Dew would be a sick yellowy-green).

- that the real reason ostriches stick their heads in the sand is to search for water?
(and that Osama and his men use this same technique).

- that Humphry Bogart was related to Princess Diana?
(Humphry once smoked one of Diana's great-uncle's discarded stogies).

- that the first Harley Davidson motorcycle built in 1903 used a tomato can for a carburetor?

(and twenty-five years later Ford finally caught on to the idea and have been using it ever since).

- that when you sneeze, all bodily functions stop including your heart?
  (if you sneeze twenty times in a row like I am prone to do, your brain could conceivably be without oxygen for several minutes causing brain damage. Hmmmm...)

- that the average person will spend seven years of his/her life waiting in lines?
  (I spend seven years in lines every Christmas Season!)

- that in most TV commercials they use white paint and paint thinner instead of real milk?
  (and more and more people are beginning to prefer their cereal this way. They say that their morning bowl of cereal puts a smile on their face and that they find it much easier to head out to work every morning, and most don't remember how they got there!)

- that I am now finished with this segment.
  (thank goodness!)

Nursery Stories
(Rated x)

Do you remember the nursery story about the brother and sister, Hansel and Gretel? Or did your parents not expose you to such violence.

If you've never read or heard this story, here is a condensed version:

- Hansel and Gretel are little children
- They were abused by their mean stepfather
- They run away from home
- They wander through the forest and stumble upon a witch's house
- The witch offers them food and invites them in
- She traps them, locks them in a cage, and prepares to cook them for her supper
- A bird helps them to escape by opening the cage door
- The children sneak up on the witch and push her into the fireplace where she dies an awful death

- A woodcutter (lumberjack in Canada), follows their trail of bread crumbs that they dropped so as to not get lost, and rescues them
- They tell him their story
- The woodcutter (lumberjack in Canada) takes Hansel and Gretel home and chops off the head of the wicked step-father and then marries the children's mother
- They all live happily ever after!

Now, would you read this story to your little child or grandchild just before he or she goes to sleep?

What's **wrong** with this story?

1)   child abuse
2)   child neglect
3)   unlawful confinement
4)   kidnapping
5)   littering
6)   attempted cannibalism
7)   practice of witchcraft
8)   murder of the witch
9)   murder of the stepfather
10)   marriage of mother to murderer
11)   happy ending

Hollywood should make a movie about this! It could make a successful action packed horror movie starring Arnold Schwarzenegger as the woodcutter (lumberjack in Canada) and Jack Nicholson as the crazed maniacal stepfather.

My personal all time favorite children's story was "Jack and the Beanstalk". I had this story on a viewmaster disc. The pictures were so vivid, and the giant so mean and terrible looking, that I would scare myself half to death every time I looked at it!

But now that I think about this story, I realize that **Jack** was the true villain of this story and **not** the giant!

Firstly, Jack **disobeyed** his mother who told him to sell their only cow to get some money to buy food. Jack, besides being disobedient, was also quite **dopey** as he traded the cow for three "magic"beans. If this story had taken place in North America, he probably would have traded the cow for a couple of acres of swampland in Florida.

Next, he **trespasses** on the giant's property. Then he carries out a **B&E** (break & enter) on the giant's castle while the giant is away.

Then he commits **theft** of over $5,000 when he steals a magic harp and a hen that lays golden eggs.

And finally he **murders** the giant who is just trying to get his possessions back.

This makes one heck of a rap sheet!

Then Jack and his mother have the gall to live happily ever after!

Don't you feel just a tiny bit sorry for the

giant? He was just minding his own business living in his castle up in the clouds until Jack showed up, breaking into his castle, stealing from him, and eventually killing him.

The story doesn't give the details about how the giant's wife and baby giants had to carry on without him, while Jack and his mother "lived happily ever after" with their stolen magic harp and golden egg laying goose. The giant family in fact, "suffered ever after" because of the villainous rogue, Jack.

"Fee, fie, fo, fum,
Jack's a villain,
And so's his mum."
The end.

Good Luck!

There are many people around the world who are extremely superstitious. Some won't even leave their homes on the infamous Friday the Thirteenth. The clinical name to describe those who fear Friday the Thirteenth is something like "Paraskevidekatriaphobia".

I for one am not superstitious in the least. In fact, when I played highschool football my jersey number was thirteen. I was wearing this jersey when the nurses at the hospital cut it off me after I arrived with a dislocated hip. I still have this jersey. My teammates presented it to me while I was in the hospital recovering. I now have it mounted on my bedroom wall as well as on the wall in my rec room.

There are hundreds of phobias that cover almost every abnormal fear that there could possibly be. Following are some of the most common:

Claustrophobia	-fear of being closed in
Acrophobia	-fear of heights
Arachnophobia	-fear of spiders
Hydrophobia	-fear of water
Agoraphobia	-fear of open spaces
Herpetophobia	-fear of reptiles

Following is a list of **not** so well known phobias that may be new to you:

Frangaphobia	-fear of kitchen utensils
Saritaphobia	-fear of men with bad comb-overs
Pireaphobia	-fear of women wearing corduroy pants starting fires
Zippitydoodaphobia	-fear of being sickeningly cheerful
Mexiphobia	-fear of tacos
Gyseraphobia	-fear of unexpected eruption while changing a baby boy's diaper
Sombrerophobia	-fear of someone complimenting you on your new and unusual hat when actually you are just having a "bad hair day"
Brewskiphobia	-fear of someone spilling their beer over you at a hockey game
Yelpaphobia	-fear of receiving a wedgie
Bowlegaphobia	-fear of falling in love with a cello player

Glazeophobia	-fear of dropping and breaking a mirror and receiving seven years bad luck
Uglymugaphobia	-fear of breaking a mirror with your reflection and being mistaken for Quasimoto for seven years
Liberaceophobia	-fear of a grand piano falling eleven stories and landing on your head
Pronounced Liberaceophobia	-fear of being <u>dressed like</u> Liberace when hit on the head by a grand piano
Snoozaphobia	-fear of people falling asleep while you are speaking to them (this phobia is especially prominent among men and women of the cloth)
GomerPileaphobia	-fear of Jim

Neighbours com-
ing out with a new
CD called "A Pile
of Rap"

If you should suffer from any of these afflic-
tions, you have my sympathy, and I recommend
that you see a psychiatrist as soon as possible. (If
you are not too afraid to do so, that is!)

Gesundheit!

Why don't we ever sneeze in our sleep? I don't know about you, but this has never happened to me. I have never woken myself up sneezing. I mean if you have to sneeze you have to sneeze, right? Do our cilia take a break when we fall asleep? Can we not sneeze unless our brain first tells us that it is OK to do so? Is it because there would be no one around to bless us? (Except of course your spouse who would probably not care to heap many blessings on you for blowing them out of bed at four o'clock in the morning!)

Just stop and think how dangerous this would be. If sleeping on your stomach, you would first inhale half of your pillow before sneezing it back out. (Although it *would* serve as a handy handkerchief and muffler!)

If sleeping on your side facing your spouse, he or she would receive a very rude awakening as you shower him or her, and scare the wits out of them with the thunderous explosion.

If you are on your back, you could cause yourself serious injury as you lurch upward, deep in sleep, arching your back and actually rising six inches off of the mattress as you blow your brains out.

If this doesn't wake you, you will probably be wondering when you awake in the morning why you are suffering from whiplash or why your back is out.

As far as I am concerned it is a very good thing that we do not sneeze in our sleep. Isn't it amazing how we have these built-in anti-destruction mechanisms programmed in us?

Left or Right Headed

I have never fully understood the "left and right side of the brain" stuff. My limited understanding of it is that the left side of the brain is used for the logical, analytical, pragmatic, and hedonistic personality traits of an individual, while the right side is used for the compassionate, creative, and sensitive personality traits of the individual.

They say that men use the left side of the brain more often than the right side, and for the most part use one side at a time. Meanwhile, women seem to have more of a balance between the left and right side, and can use both sides at the same time.

This would certainly explain how women can talk to a friend on the telephone and read a book at the same time, while men don't seem to be able to concentrate on what their wives are saying to them while they are watching hockey.

These differences in usage of the brain can create considerable havoc in the home. Let's take last night for example... I need something. I look for it in the place where it is normally always kept. It isn't there. The left side of my brain says, "We're all out of this stuff. There is no more left". I then very calmly say to my wife, "Dear, we are all out of this stuff."

To which she answers, "We are not! I just bought some the other day!"

Very sweetly I remark, "But there's none here! The kids must have used it all up!"

Then she screams, "Just open your eyes and look for it! It's there!"

I quietly respond, "I'm sorry, dear, but we don't have any!"

She then threatens, "If I come in there and find it, you're in big trouble!"

She then shoves me aside and looks for the object in a completely foreign place, a place where I would never expect this thing to be. Then the degrading remarks begin. "You're as blind as a bat! You need glasses! Typical man!" She then calls to all of our children and anyone else who happens to be in our house at the time, or walking by our house outside, to show them how easy this item was to locate and that *I* couldn't find it.

For men, it is logical that everything has a time and a place in life. Women have to mix in stuff from "that other side of the brain" to confuse and complicate issues.

Man: (thinking to himself before going grocery shopping with his wife)

"Let's see now... if we leave here by 6:30 we can be there by 6:48. It usually takes about 1 hour and 45 minutes to shop. By the time we load up the car, drive back, and unload, I should be in my chair at 8:30 when the game starts."

Woman: (thinking to herself before going grocery shopping with her husband)
"Gee, I haven't spoken to Marge in over a week."

While in the store the wife bumps into eight different people that she knows. She stops to reminisce with each of them while her husband hides-out in the cold cut section hoping that no one he knows will spot him. She stops for eleven minutes to read a magazine. She uses up valuable seconds looking at stuff that she doesn't need or can't afford.

The husband by now is a nervous wreck! Ulcers begin to develop. Hair begins to fall out! The game has already started and he is still standing in line at the checkout! And everyone wonders why most husbands pass on before their wives!

The Gift of Life

My wife and I once volunteered to give blood at the Red Cross a long time ago. We were just newly married and thought that this would be a decent thing to do.

As we arrived, they first typed us. My wife possesses a very common blood type. I, of course, possess an extremely rare blood type. If I ever require a transfusion, I was notified that they would have to fly in a member of the Objudu (pronounced 'Tkeptza') tribe of central Tanzania. All members of this tribe apparently have this rare blood type. This blood type is also known to be quite common in hobos.

We were next led to recliner chairs and were told that this should take between five to ten minutes, after which we could rest awhile and have coffee and donuts.

I was done in about five minutes. After my fourth donut and third cup of coffee I began to wonder why my wife wasn't joining me. Knowing her, I figured that she was probably in the laboratory with the nurse helping to analyze the samples.

When I finally asked my wife's whereabouts, the nurse told me that she wasn't finished giving blood yet.

After an hour and a half had elapsed, I was sick of donuts and was sloshing around like a beached whale on a caffeine high. I got up and went to check on my wife. She was still in the recliner. She was as pale as Casper the ghost. The pint bag she was trying to fill was still half-empty. There were three nurses working on her trying to help pump the blood out. One nurse had hold of her arm and was pumping it up and down like a handle on a lift pump. Another had straddled her and was massaging her heart while a third was waving smelling salts under her nose.

As 5:00 P.M. rolled around, we were told that we had to leave because they were closing and they were out of donuts. My wife's pint bag was not quite filled yet, but they told her that it was OK and that she gave it a "nice try". They then gave her coupons to visit at a later date to receive her free donuts and coffee, but not to donate blood.

We haven't been back since. They have never called my wife since. They have called me a few times when the occasion has arisen that a hobo passing through town has fallen out of a railway car and needed an immediate transfusion.

I wear a bracelet around my wrist that says that if I am ever in need of a transfusion, that railyards should be checked first before sending a safari to Tanzania.

Do any of you happen to have type "Special-K Negative?" If you do, I want to be your friend!

I Thought You'd Might Like to Know

Who **wouldn't** want to know where the expression "Everything is Hunky-Dory" originated? I can't believe that there would be anybody alive or dead who would not want to know this.

I recently spent several minutes fully researching this peculiar phrase. It was time well spent, however, as its historical background is quite phenomenal.

This phrase's origin dates back to the First World War. Russia, back then, did not particularly care all too much for the Ukrainian Province, and treated the Ukrainians with disdain. They were treated as second-class citizens. (Which still wasn't all **that** bad considering that there existed fourteen classes of people in Russia at the time).

As you are most probably aware, there exists an indiscreet slang for the people of Ukrainian descent, namely 'Hunky'.

During the war, when a Russian Navy vessel would approach an area where mines were detected, the Russian sailors would put a Ukrainian or two into a row boat (dory), and make them row through the mined waters. The larger vessel would follow at a safe distance. If the rowboat and its crew happened to get blown out of the water after being struck by a mine, the Russian vessel would detour around that area, and very quickly get another 'Hunky' into the water.

As long as the dory, and the Hunky rowing it, were still afloat and moving, there therefore remained a "Hunky in the dory".

So the phrase today still carries the meaning that everything is A-OK when "Everything is Hunky dory".

White Collar Games

Down in Idaho, there is an event held annually called the "Red Neck Olympics". You know, the cow-pie throwing, cherry pit spitting, tractor pulling, and pie eating type of events that are a real 'turn-on' for dedicated Red Necks. Not only are some of these events just downright silly, there oftentimes is insufficient coordination in the planning of the events.

For example, at last year's games the pole-climbing event had just gotten under way when one of the officials of the games shot his starting pistol to commence the tree-cutting event. The tree-cutting contestants won this event as they managed to saw through the two poles while the pole-climbing contestants had just started to make their descents on them. There were, however, new world records set for the pole-climbing event as the two contestant's rates of descent were incredibly swift.

Up here in Canada, we tend to be a tad more on the refined side. We are more reserved.

For instance, did you know there is actually an annual "White Collar Games" that is held in a different city in Canada every summer? It's not very well publicized, which is too bad because I am sure numerous office-type people like myself would be very interested when the games came to our respective locales.

In case you may be interested and would like more information on the annual "Canadian White Collar Games", I will briefly provide a list of some of the events that take place at the games. Maybe a few of us more serious white-collar athletic types may consider going into training for one or more of the events.

OFFICE CHAIR RACE

Teams of two contestants each, with one sitting in the chair and the other pushing it, race around a veledrome track. There are no rules for this event other than everyone has to travel in the same direction and the male participants must wear suits, ties, and leather dress shoes.

ACCELERATED PENCIL SHARPENING

Contestants must use a manual pencil sharpener and must sharpen the full length of a pencil right down to the eraser in the fastest possible time. The current world record holder in this event is Lefty Simms from Beaver Creek, Nova Scotia, with a time of 11.2 seconds.

CALCULATOR TOSS

A cordless, desktop size calculator is held in discus-like fashion. The competitor spins one and a half revolutions and tosses the calculator for distance. The defending champion in this event is Murray Kowalski, a five foot ten inch, two hundred and forty-three pound account- ant from Moose Jaw, Saskatchewan, who dis- covered his talent for hurling calculators after numerous attempts at trying to balance his year end inventory in 1971.

THE NEUTRALIZER

Competitors sit on an office chair with paper cutters on their laps. (Manual cutters with handle and blade) They must slice an overly ripe zucchini into the most possible pieces in the shortest possible time. Females pri- marily dominate this event, as the male con- testants tend to be overly cautious.

THE MAILER

Contestants must fold and stuff three hun- dred and fifty pieces of advertising material into envelopes in the shortest period of time. This event carries the most casualties of the games as paper cuts abound. In 1981 a novice secretary from Wawa, Ontario, Selma Cunningham, required a blood transfusion fol- lowing this event.

THE SHREDDER

Three reams of paper must be put through a shredder in the fastest possible time. Paper jams are totally the responsibility of the contest- ant. Proper business attire is, of course required.

Men must wear suits and ties. Blouses with long sleeves and necklaces and other jewelry are required for women. Tie jams and blouse, hair, finger, or jewelry jams are also totally the responsibility of the contestants.

THE 400 METER RELAY

Men or women in teams of four and dressed in full business attire, run a distance of 100 meters each before passing a briefcase holding worthless documents to their teammate. It is therefore very similar to any other competitive relay race except at the finish line where the teammate designated as the "anchor" (usually the team member with the shortest name), must sit behind a desk, open the briefcase, and sign the documents included therein. The first pen to hit the desktop after the documents are signed signifies the winning team.

THE FIVE O'CLOCK DASH

In a mock office setting, at the sound of the starter's pistol, the contestants must shut down all of their equipment, turn off all of the lights, lock all doors, put on coats, run to their vehicles, unlock the door and get in (no automatic door openers or starters are permitted). The first to cross the finish line at the parking lot exit is the winner.

The current record holder in this event is Todd, "the clockwatcher", Neufeld, a shipping clerk from Lively, Ontario, with a record time of 12.56 seconds.

WATER COOLER BLITZ

Competitors must cover a distance of fifty yards carrying a ten-gallon jug of water under each arm. The first to reach the cooler at the finish line and install one of the jugs, is the winner.

"Gorilla" Moscovitz, a bulldozer salesman from, Try to Find This Here Cove, New Brunswick, set a new world's record last year of 13.76 seconds.

THE DECATHLON

The decathlon is by far the most difficult and grueling event of the "White Collar Games". Contestants must run a distance of one mile with a telephone receiver cradled between their jaw and shoulder, carrying a cup of coffee in one hand and a briefcase in the other. Keeping the telephone receiver cradled, they must then cycle another mile, stopping at three locations along the route to drink a cup of coffee at each. The final leg of the race is the one hundred-meter dash to the washroom at the finish line.

If you are interested in attending these games when they come to your area, look for the notice of "The Canadian White Collar Games" in the Business Section of your local newspaper.

CHITTY CHITTY CLUNK CLUNK

I have yet to own a brand new vehicle. I just cannot bring myself to commit to that kind of monstrous debt and to using my children for collateral. Besides, now that they are all grown up, they are viewed more as liabilities than as assets.

I have come across articles in magazines on several occasions pointing out the fact that the most economical route to take in purchasing a vehicle, in the long run, is to purchase a used one and drive it until it expires, and then abandon it. You must of course make an effort to maintain it to the best of your financial ability, which in my case amounts to putting gas in it once in awhile. So for example, the recommendation is to purchase a vehicle that is four to eight years old and drive it until the cost of fixing it exceeds the value of it. This is the practice that I have chosen to follow over the past thirty-five years. I may be further ahead in the long run financially, but I certainly have suffered mentally and emotionally over these years.

It all started when I was twenty years old and purchased my very first car. It was a beauty! It was a 1966 Valiant Signet, white with red interior, bucket seats, and it had a motor in the front. I paid six hundred dollars for it.

One summer Saturday afternoon, I came outside, hopped into my Signet, and began moving out of my parking stall when I discovered that I had no breaks. Nothing! There had been no indication, no warning that the breaks were problematic. I knew that I had to get my car to a service station for repairs, but I also knew that I had very little money in my bank account. No way was I going to pay for a tow truck to tow me to the nearest service station some eight blocks away!

It was at this point that I solicited the help of my wife Dawn, who was my girlfriend at the time. We devised a plan that we would put into operation the following morning. As the traffic would be lighter on Sunday morning, I decided that the two of us working in tandem, could accomplish this mission of getting my car *sans brakes,* to the service station eight blocks away in one piece, without being involved in an accident, or at the very least, without getting killed.

We traveled the alleyways as much as possible. Dawn would jog ahead of me as I drove at idle speed. At intersections she would use hand signals to alert me if there was a vehicle approaching or if the coast was clear. If there was danger ahead, I would slip the transmission into neutral and coast, hopefully to a stop, before entering the intersection.

Amazingly, all went well. We arrived at our

destination safely, albeit quite flustered by the mental anguish and stress.

As the service station was closed, being Sunday, I called the following morning to identify my car and myself. When asked by the mechanic what the problem was, I simply stated "the brakes".

When picking my car up later that same day, the mechanic appeared quite short and flustered with me as he barked, "Why didn't you tell me that the brakes were completely gone?" Apparently, when attempting to turn my car around in order to drive it forward into the service bay, he had backed it out of the lot onto the street. Imagine his surprise when his foot drove the brake pedal unimpeded to the floorboard! He then went on to explain how fortunate I was that no traffic was behind him when he exercised this maneuver. The curb on the opposite side of the street is what stopped his backward momentum.

While settling my bill I casually mentioned to him that **he too** was fortunate, considering the fact that he didn't heed my direction that "the brakes" were the problem.

A few years later, now happily married and planning a family, my wife and I decided that it was time to purchase a newer, more practical vehicle. After some shopping around we came across a potentially terrific deal for a great family car. We told the salesman that we would like to "think about it" overnight and that we would give him our answer the following day.

Well, we decided to buy this 1975 Dodge Dart, four door, economical family car. I called the salesman and told him that we were on our way down to sign the deal. Part of the deal was the trade-in of our present car. No value had yet been set on our little Valiant. As it was in the month of February and quite cold, Dawn and I bundled up and left our apartment for the parking lot. We climbed into our Signet. I placed the key into the ignition and turned it. E-r-r-r-r-r-e-r-r-r-r-r, e-r-r-r-r-r-e-r-r-r-r-r ping, ping. Silence followed. "No, this *can't* be happening! Not now! Gimme a break!" I cried. I tried starting it up a couple more times before the battery went completely dead. What were we to do now? We headed back up to our apartment where I immediately called my elder brother and explained the situation. He calmly replied that he would be right over.

Our Signet started up after boosting the battery. My brother generously volunteered to follow us on our drive to the car dealership some four miles away, in case we ran into anymore problems. Well, we did. At every traffic light that I was forced to stop at, the old Signet sputtered and sighed to a stall. Each time this happened my brother would pull up along side of us, hook up the cables and boost us into motion. It took us over an hour to cover the four miles to the dealership.

As we turned into the dealership's lot, I waved good-bye and thank you to my brother who continued on his way. As I began slowing down to park, we stalled once again. While coasting into the parking stall, I prayed that our salesman, who had spotted us arrive and was already making his way toward us, did not notice that the engine had ceased to run before we had completely stopped moving and without me turning the ignition off.

After the paperwork had been completed, Dawn and I very proudly and joyously jumped into our "new" car. Glancing into my rear view mirror as I approached the exit, I watched as our salesman climbed into our Signet in order to move it from the front lot to the service bays around back. E-r-r-r-r-r-r, e-r-r-r-r-r-r-r, ping, ping!

We loved our 1975 Dodge Dart and drove it until it was fifteen years old. It probably could have been good for a few more years, but it began to become a safety hazard when items that were inside, began to 'osmote' to the outside, through the holes rusted throughout seventy-five percent of the body and floor.

Another hazardous thing that our Dart would do was to stall in the middle of left-hand turns. If we were making a right hand turn, which is fairly safe to do, there would be no problem. But when we had to turn left, and cross the path of oncoming traffic, our Dart would quite often stall. The chain of events would progress as such: light turns green, I move to the centre of the intersection, there is oncoming traffic, I wait, I see a break, I accelerate, I begin to move but then the engine stalls, oncoming traffic is bearing down on me, I slip the transmission into neutral, I begin to coast through the intersection, oncoming traffic begins blowing horns, I begin to sweat, "am I going to make it to safety, or am I going to die here? If I am hit, will the other vehicle 'osmote' through the porous, rusted body? Will *I* 'osmote' through the porous, rusted body?" Then while still rolling, I would turn the ignition, which would fire up the engine and allow us to continue on our way.

It was at this point that I attempted several different methods to see if I could entice someone to steal our car so that I could collect something on the insurance. I would leave it abandoned in parking lots for days. I would leave it on the street with the motor running, doors unlocked and windows open, but that didn't work. (I had to leave the motor running because unless he knew how to jiggle the key *just right* in the ignition, the average thief would never be able to start it).

We eventually sold our beloved rusted-out Dart to a Manitoba farmer for six hundred dollars. He apparently owned a fleet of similar types of vehicles and was quite happy to have come across this "steal of a deal".

Because our Dart was a standard model with virtually no optional equipment other than a radio, we decided that our next vehicle should be "fully loaded" with amenities. And it was! Our 1982 Oldsmobile Delta 88 **was** "fully loaded". My entire family enjoyed these many wonderful options for several months until they began, one by one, to malfunction.

The first to go were the power doors and windows. Having the windows up all winter long did not create any problems, but in the sweltering Manitoba summers, the windows magnified the sun's rays roasting the incarcerated passengers to near death. Using the drive-through at McDonald's also proved to be a challenge as I would have to clamber out the door to place my order, and again when I picked it up and paid for it.

Air conditioning? Yes. Yes we had it, and yes it didn't work. When the hot temperatures of summer came upon us our A/C began blowing hot air, and of course in winter it blew cold air.

A few of the other optional electrical and mechanical gadgets that ceased to function shortly after purchasing the Olds were: the cigarette lighter, the trunk lid release, the cruise control, the speedometer, the hydraulic contraption that holds the trunk lid up, and the horn.

The windshield wipers also malfunctioned. Oftentimes I would exit my house on a bright, sunny summer morning and climb into the Olds and start her up. Oftentimes the windshield wipers would be set into motion at the same instant the engine started up. The wipers **were not** turned to the "on" position. They **hadn't been left on** and I **had not turned them on**. But they **were on** and I **could not turn them off**.

Oftentimes Dawn and I would drive all the way to work on a bright, sunny, summer morning, with the windshield wipers slapping out their happy-go-lucky rhythm. This became especially embarrassing when stopped at traffic lights. Drivers on each side of us would gape through our non-functioning closed windows, wondering why we had our wipers on, and why we had beads of sweat on our brows. Sometimes I would spray the window with washer fluid in order to pretend that I was actually washing my windshield. This attempt to fool them didn't work for long after having to pull up along side the same drivers for several red lights in succession, and proceeding to wash my windshield each time.

If **this** wiper problem weren't enough then **this** would be. Oftentimes the wipers on the Olds **did not work in the rain**. Sometimes the visibility would get so poor that I would have been better off to stick my head out of the window to see what was in front of me. That is, of course, if I could have managed to get the window to go down.

So far I have not touched upon the subject of the motor and other contrivances under the hood or under the car itself. Why is it that when I went to have a new muffler installed I would see signs all around the city advertising, "Mufflers, $25.88 guaranteed for the life of your car", but because of the make, model, year and colour of my Olds it would cost me $125.88

with no guarantee. When I asked about the "guarantee for the life of your car", I was told that my car had no life.

Why is it that women get so paranoid about little insignificant car problems? When driving with my wife she is constantly saying such things as, "I smell something burning!" or "What's that smoke?" or "Do you hear that noise? It doesn't sound very good!"

I have a solution to all such questions. When you begin to **smell** something burning, immediately open your window, if you can, to allow the draft to remove the obnoxious smell. As soon as you **see** a hint of smoke, immediately roll your window up to keep the smoke from entering your car. And if you begin to **hear** pinging or clunking noises, immediately turn the volume up on your radio or tape deck. These actions when done quickly can usually prevent comments from your wife, which may cost you a lot of time and money to get this stuff fixed. That is **my** definition of 'preventative maintenance'.

My wife and I used to joke sometimes about how our vehicle was virtually theft proof. We didn't require "The Club" or any similar type security apparatus, and besides that, we never had to lock our doors or close our windows, that is, if we actually could have opened our windows in the first place.

Firstly, our Olds by this time did not **look** like the kind of vehicle that anyone would want to risk a prison term for by trying to steal it. Then the thief would have to deal with trying to start it. With or without the key this would be quite challenging. Even if the thief managed to get as far as starting it up, after a mile or so the white smoke that always filtered through the firewall would soon begin filling the interior. As the thief would try in vain to roll the windows down, his eyes would then begin to burn from the smoke. As he would attempt to get his bearings as to whether he was traveling on the right side of the road or not, the windshield wipers would come on, further hampering his ability to see where he was going. He would then glance down at the limp speedometer, which would offer no glimpse of how fast he was traveling.

If the police had not stopped him by now due to his erratic driving, they would certainly stop him for not using his turn signals, which also did not work. Or maybe some "Good Samaritan" would eventually flag him down to notify him that one of his wheelcovers had detached from the wheel and was already a block ahead of him heading West. Heaven forbid if the thief ever tried to put anything into the trunk. The trunk lid must have weighed in the vicinity of one hundred and fifty pounds, and after lifting it, if he let it go without supporting it with the hockey stick shaft supplied, it would probably be the last thing he would have done here on earth.

One day at work, one of the employees sent an e-mail to all the staff asking if anyone was interested in purchasing an automatic car starter at a very good price. I answered him back stating that my car didn't start when I was in it, let alone if I was at some remote location.

So what have I learned after all of these years? Absolutely nothing! I still cannot afford to purchase a brand-new car, and will continue to purchase vehicles that are just on the verge of massive breakdowns after their original owners are done with them.

Looking on the bright side of things, I have made many new friends over the years thanks to my cars. After all these years, I continue to send and to receive Christmas cards from most of the motor league employees. I am even the Godfather to two of their youngsters.

Like I said at the outset, I have probably saved thousands of dollars over the years, which greatly helps to offset the cost of the medication that I keep in the glove compartment and on which I have become to be so dependent.

Groundhog Day

Why don't we have a ceremony for Groundhog Day in Winnipeg to determine how much longer winter will be?

Is it because we are afraid that the little rodent will tell us that we will have six more months on top of the six that we've just endured? Or maybe it's because the little varmint wouldn't even make the effort to show his snout until May.

Here is my suggestion:

On February 2 of each year at exactly 9:00 A.M., the mayor of Winnipeg would come out onto the steps of City Hall and promptly plant his tongue on the iron railing. If he can't dislodge it by himself within five minutes and requires assistance from the fire department, it would mean that winter would last another month. If on the other hand, he can't dislodge it, **but** at the same time can still address the crowd and media with a discernible speech, then who cares about winter anyway? Watching this event take place every year would be **worth** another month, or even several more months of winter.

Did you ever get your tongue stuck on a metal object as a kid in the winter? How about as an adult?

There are always those nasty kids in the schoolyard who try to persuade unsuspecting younger kids to "lick the flagpole" in January, explaining that it is one of the most patriotic things that a proud Canadian can do.

I never did this. Taunting younger kids to do anything so ridiculous, that is. I did however get myself into somewhat of a dilemma once when I was nine years old. Showing off, as usual, to my friends and a group of girls waiting at a bus stop in the middle of winter, I reckoned that I had to go one step better than one of my friends who decided to kiss the metal pole of the bus stop. He received such adulation and laughter by doing this that I just had to quickly find a way to top his performance.

Now I don't recommend that anyone try this, unless you are in very good physical condition like I was when I was nine years old.

When the next bus arrived and stopped, I strolled to the rear of it and casually called out to the boys and girls still waiting there, "O yeh! Well watch **this**!" I then placed my tongue on the back end of the bus. I was very surprised at how quickly my tongue permanently attached to the metal. As the bus pulled away from the stop, I ran behind managing to keep up amid the laughing and cheering of the delighted crowd.

I only had to travel a block or so affixed to the bus, as a passing motorist noticed my dilemma and flagged it down. The bus driver then administered some of his coffee to help detach me from the metal monster.

I survived this experience none the worse for wear except that I had to abstain from eating and drinking hot and cold things for a few weeks following. I also had no appetite in the least for all day suckers!

Ye-e-e-e-e-e-e-r' Out!

I am not an avid baseball fan, so I need someone to explain to me why the training camp for the Major Leagues opens in February. Why do these guys need two months to get ready for a two hundred game season?

Canadian football has a two-week training camp, followed by two exhibition games before they formally start the eighteen game regular season.

If you ask me, football is a much more complex and detailed game that requires terrific conditioning. Because there are so few games played in a season, every single game is of paramount importance.

The same holds true for hockey. A two-week training camp is followed by a dozen exhibition games and then a season of eighty-four games. Again, incredible conditioning is required.

Now baseball on the other hand, requires little conditioning. Other than the pitchers' arms, the rest of the team can stay in condition during the off-season simply by jogging a little each day, and doing a little weight training. That's it! That's all they need! But **n-o-o-o-o-o-o**! They play a two hundred game season. Each game on an individual basis is not all that crucial. The sport is so physically undemanding that they can play two games one after the other, and can play five games in three days.

What kinds of strategies does the team need to practice? As long as the manager knows what's going on, he can let the rest of the team know. The game moves **s-o-o-o-o** slowly, that he can let them know everything that they have to do. They don't even have to think for themselves.

Example:

A player goes up to bat. The manager in the dugout signals the third base coach what he wants the batter to do. The third base coach then relays the manager's message to the batter. (I don't know why the manager just can't tell the batter what he wants him to do before he leaves the dugout. Is he afraid that he might forget on his way to the batter's box?) The batter then tries to follow through with the instructions given him. If he manages to get a hit, the manager will signal the first base coach what to do. The first base coach will then tell the runner what to do.

Meanwhile, the **other** team's manager signals from **his** dugout to his infield and outfield, where he wants them to position themselves, and what to do. He then signals the catcher who in turn signals the pitcher, as to what pitch to throw. The right fielder then signals one of the players in the bullpen that he needs more chewing tobacco.

Now remember, if any of these signals gets crossed, they simply call a time-out so that they can get everything straightened away. The manager yells, "Time-Out!" and casually strolls from the dugout out to the pitcher's mound. The infielders will then stroll over to the pitcher's mound. The catcher joins in and strolls over to the pitcher's mound. The home plate umpire goes for a beer. Hundreds of fans head for the washroom.

Why do they need two months of training and conditioning camp? Is it so that the managers can practice to become proficient at kicking dirt? Is it so that the players can practice blowing bubbles with their bubble gum? Is it so that the players can practice their timing so that they will spit and adjust themselves at the exact second the television camera or Jumbotron camera is on them? Is it for the players to deal drugs in the dugout? Is it for managers to practice their cussing and screaming into the umpires' faces?

You see, what actually happens is that each team has several blow-up umpires that are positioned around the field during training camp. Every once in a while the manager will storm out onto the field, kick some dirt at it, put his face right up against the umpire's rubber face, and scream and cuss. The manager will then retire back to the dugout to rest a bit before repeating his raucous, abusive tirade.

The more practice he can muster up, the more diverse his performances can be, and therefore become more of a fan favorite.

Don't you really think that all of this could be accomplished during a two- week period, with just ten exhibition games? How much **more ready** are the players after two months of training and fifty exhibition games? How many **more** of the two hundred games that they play during the season will they win? What difference can it possibly make?

I realize that I have probably offended quite a number of avid baseball fans by now, and if they could have their way they would toss me out of the game. So I will just quietly 'hit the showers' now.

You Are What You Eat
(I guess that makes me a hot dog)

Why do most foods that are the best for us taste the worst, and the foods that are worst for us taste the best?

I wonder about this a lot. Pizza, hot dogs, soft drinks, potato chips, chocolate, KFC, and other fast foods, are not the best things that one can put into his or her body. But why can't spinach, broccoli, turnips, liver, etc. taste good?

Don't tell me it's because of the sugar content in desserts and candy. If you covered any vegetable or liver in chocolate sauce it still wouldn't taste like a pecan pie!

"Eating healthy" unfortunately, means eating the stuff you don't like.

I hear so often about different foods tasting like chicken. Frog legs, rabbit, snake, porcupine, apparently all taste like chicken. So my question is, why can't chicken taste like a Whopper? Why can't turnip taste like French fries? Why can't zucchini taste like cotton candy? Why can't roast beef taste like frankfurters?

If all the fast foods were invented so that they would "taste good" to the consumer, then their inventors did an excellent job in succeeding to do this.

Given my choice I would select pizza, fries, hot dogs, hamburgers, potato chips, chicken fingers, desserts, or candy over any other "natural" type food.

Why is this?

The inventors of fast foods must have discovered what tastes best to, and is craved by, most human beings. Why can't we go through a McDonald's drive through and order liver on a bun with a side order of green beans with a cup of tomato juice? Too expensive? No ! Too difficult to make? No! Problem with supply? No! It's because it would taste crappy and no one would order it, that's why!

Do you usually drink coke with your hot dog, hamburger or pizza, or do you drink milk? Do you like coffee or tea (i.e., caffeine) in the morning or a glass of nice cold, sour grapefruit juice?

What are the reasons? Taste, of course!

Think about how easy it would be to get children to eat healthy and not have to fight with them to eat their meals, if the stuff that we **wanted** them to eat tasted like the stuff that we **don't want** them to eat!

At the dinner table...

Little Tommy:	"Mom, are there any Brussel sprouts left?"
Mother:	"Tommy, if you eat one

more Brussel sprout you'll
burst!"

Tommy: "Well then, are you going
to finish your scalloped
potatoes? And by the
way, can you please pack
a salad in my lunch-box
tomorrow?"

At the movie theatre concession stand...

"I'll have the extra large box of sprouts, a
carrot and bottled water, please".

I brought some fruit and some chocolate to
work with me today. Guess which one I will eat
first? Guess which one I will enjoy the most?
Guess which one will kill me the quickest? Case
closed!
Quick, pass the pizza pops!

Ring My Chimes

Around one hundred and twenty-five years ago, the great Russian psychologist Pavlov, completed his experiments on "conditioned reflex training".

The premise was that when a laboratory dog did something that Pavlov wanted it to do, at the time that Pavlov wanted it to do it, he would condition the dog's behavior with a sound and then immediately reward it.

For example, if he showed the dog three cards numbered one, two, and three, and the dog touched number two with its nose, Pavlov would ring a bell and would then reward it with food.

Obviously it did not take the dog very long to figure out that the number two was its lucky number. No matter how Pavlov mixed these numbers up, the dog would always select the number two.

Pavlov was so successful with these experiments that he decided to try the "conditioned reflex" technique on a human, namely his wife Helga.

Now he didn't **tell** Helga what he was up to because it would affect the control factor of his experiment.

Everytime that Helga would get up early in the morning and make Pavlov's favorite breakfast, cabbage and goose eggs, Pavlov would ring a bell and give her a flower.

It worked! Very soon thereafter, Pavlov just had to ring the bell whenever he had a hankering for cabbage and goose eggs and it would be served to him tout suite, no questions asked.

Everything went along quite nicely for a few months with Pavlov enjoying his regular menu of cabbage and goose eggs, and Helga receiving many beautiful flowers.

Then one day Pavlov decided to try to elicit a conditioned reflex from Helga in the evening, instead of early in the morning. It was at this point that Helga finally caught on to her husband's "experiment". She became very upset with Pavlov and rang **his** bell and directed him to the couch.

After several weeks of silence, and sleeping on the couch, Pavlov decided to put his life on the line. The next morning he began ringing the bell to see what would happen.

As he lay on the couch for a few minutes not knowing what to expect, he suddenly smelled the sweet aroma of cabbage and goose eggs cooking in the kitchen.

He smiled to himself.

He lit a cigarette.

When he finished his smoke, the delicious aroma was just too much for him to bear any longer. He made his way to the kitchen with love in his heart and an appetite in his belly. And there in the kitchen dishing up a serving of cabbage and goose eggs done to perfection, was Pavlov's dog, Fidov!

MORALS OF THIS STORY...

Don't count your goose eggs before they're hatched.

A dog is man's best friend. (especially if it can cook)

When it comes to women, keep your clapper under control.

The Longalegas

Did you know that although the sport of bungee jumping is relatively new to the civilized world, it has actually been around for centuries in the uncivilized world?

This sport originated in the Congo some four hundred and fifty years ago. As history reports, a native of the Congo was in the process of building a tree house for his family to protect them from snakes, spiders, tigers, other warring tribes, and in-laws.

Now this tree house was to be built very high up among the trees, so as a precaution the builder measured out a length of twisted vines that when tied around his ankle would stop him, if he should fall, just short of the ground, thus saving him from severe injury or even death.

As it so happened, this builder did indeed lose his balance one day and fall. The twisted vines saved his life. What was unexpected about the accident was the incredible rush that he received from the experience.

Throughout the process of building his new tree house, this particular native encountered several more 'accidents' which sent him plunging toward earth. Several times throughout the day his neighbours, who were scattered about in the village down below, would hear a scream something like, **"aaaaaYEEEEEEEEEEAAAAAaaaaaaaaaaaaaa"**.

The members of his tribe became quite accustomed to this daily occurrence, and upon hearing this scream would just utter amongst themselves that Guku was encountering another accident.

After his tree house was completed, Guku continued to have many accidents. For example, on several occasions he tripped over one of his children's toys and went flying off the edge of the stoop into a free fall swan dive. He also rolled out of bed in the middle of the night, out the door and over the edge. Guku also became a compulsive sleepwalker at this particular time of his life. Many a peaceful night's sleep of his clansmen and women was interrupted as Guku took one of his notorious three o'clock AM plunges. Because he was so accident prone, he always made sure that he had his safety vine attached to his ankle when at home, whether he was awake or at sleep.

As the other members of Guku's tribe began following his example of building their homes high above the ground in the trees for protection from in-laws, Guku impressed upon them the importance of this safety feature he had invented.

The males of the Longalegas Tribe, soon became totally engrossed in this newfound endeavor. Even after all of their homes in the trees were completed, most of their days were spent climbing the tallest trees surrounding their village with bunches of bananas on their backs. When high up above, they would tie the vines to their ankles, eat a banana, and then carefully place the peel on a branch. Then they would walk along the branches whistling to themselves while gazing skyward. All of a sudden they would unexpectedly slip on a banana peel and be sent hurling down towards the ground a hundred feet below. The vine would then snap taught, causing their brains to rattle around in their skulls producing a euphoric experience.

One evening while sitting around a fire and smoking grass, the men of the village got to talking about how it would be a good idea to ensure that all male offspring in the generations to come would also be accident prone like themselves. They decided that the best way to assure this, was that when a mother was about to give birth, the men would hoist her up a tree to a horizontal platform. If she birthed a male child, they would drop the child out of the tree while the umbilical cord was still attached, chanting prayers to the "god of the vine and clumsy accidents" the meanwhile. This ritual was to ensure that the child would always be safe from accidents in his future, but at the same time that he would experience many, many accidents during his lifetime.

The Longalegas still exist in the heart of the

Congo today, and reportedly are still as accident-prone as ever. The greatest feature about the Longalegas that sets them apart from other similarly uncivilized tribes, is that when standing on one foot the average height of the men is five feet seven inches, but when standing on the other foot their average height is six feet five inches. This makes walking somewhat cumbersome, but is a great advantage at night when dancing around the communal fire or when competing in three-legged races.

What's That You Signed?

Last evening I was watching the Parliamentary Channel on TV, (which illustrates to you the exciting life I lead), and there was this guy in the top right hand corner of the screen doing sign language for the goings on in the House of Commons.

Sign language has always amazed me. I must confess that I know absolutely nothing about it, as you will very soon attest to if you should choose to continue reading.

What happens if one of the ministers has a stutter? Is the person signing forced to do very quick repetitive movements to represent this minister accurately?

What if a shouting match develops? (Which almost always certainly does). Do the gestures of the Signer become more pronounced, more forceful, more agitated?

What does the Signer do when several ministers begin shouting at once trying to out–decibel each other? How can the Signer make it known that several people are speaking or yelling at the same time?

How do they sign a swear word without making an obscene gesture?

Do little kids who use sign language get their hands washed with soap if they sign a bad word?

How do people using sign language converse in a blackout? How can you sign, "Where are those friggin' candles!" in the pitch black?

If you were out on the golf course, how would you sign, "**Foooooooorrrre!**" before your slicing tee shot takes down a golfer on the fairway?

If you're in a restaurant and using sign language while eating, is it impolite to talk with your hands full?

Speaking of talking...

I was also at the dentist yesterday. Maybe that's why I was watching the Parliamentary Channel in the evening. I was in the mood for it!

Anyway, while I was sitting in the waiting room, I began to think that it must be terrible to be a receptionist in a dental office.

Just watching the goings on for ten minutes I noticed that patients do not want to be there. No one is in a good or talkative mood. They are probably afraid of the pain that they are about to experience or worse yet, the amount of cash that they will have to dole out to pay for their pain.

When I was leaving, I had to check in with the receptionist to make another appointment. She asked me, "Do you require another appointment?"

It was quite easy for me to answer,"Yes"even

though my entire mouth was frozen. But then she had to go and ask, "What day and time are best for you?"

Now *this* was a challenge! My tongue began to roll uncontrollably around in my mouth before sliding out and hanging down to my lower lip. Fortunately, Miss Receptionist had her eyes fixed on her computer screen and did not notice my rude gesture.

I then began to drool on the countertop. I tried to be cool as I casually wiped the spittle with my sleeve before she could notice. I then muttered something that was totally incoherent that was supposed to sound like, "Actually, any day or time next week would be fine", but it sounded more like, " Aahkuly, ana da o tie necks wee woh ba fie."

What amazes me in these situations is that they continue to do their jobs without cracking a smile. I personally would burst out laughing at this kind of stuff, but I guess they just get so used to it that it is no big deal. Unless maybe the entire staff at the dental clinic watch the security camera tape every evening after closing time. I'm sure that it would be quite entertaining. Far more entertaining than watching the parliamentary channel anyway!

"Signing off" for now

Does This Ever Happen to You?
(or are you the one who does it to me?)

Following are some personal, real-life experiences. If you have never had any of these happen to you, you are probably just not paying attention!

I go into a card shop to buy a greeting card. I'm looking for a very specific card like, "Congratulations on the success of your lobotomy". There are only a few customers in this large store. As I search for the section where I might find this particular card, lo and behold there is someone standing right in front of the section that I need to get at! They are aware that I am hovering around them. But do they step aside to read the card they are holding? Do they make any attempt to speed up their selection or to allow me access? No way!

Or, I am the only one in an entire aisle looking at cards. A customer walks into the store and immediately comes and stands directly beside me shoulder to shoulder as I browse for "In sympathy for the loss of your camel".

The next time that you are out shopping for a greeting card, pay attention and you'll see that this is true. It always happens!

When I am in a large grocery store where the aisles are very wide and spacious, and am looking for a specific item, like canned artichoke hearts in aspic, someone will invariably come along and stand beside me. They reach in front of me without excusing themselves, to grab a can from the shelf and begin reading the label first in English and then in French and then in any other language available.

I then go to the checkout. I begin to put my groceries on the moving belt. The person behind me will immediately put the little plastic stick down to separate our goods and then will jam as much of his/her groceries in the tiny vacant space as he/she possibly can. Even if this space amounts to only six inches, they will fill it. In one situation I even had the person behind me **move my stuff** in order that they could get more of their stuff on the belt. **What's the hurry?**

Whenever I go to the movies I like to get there quite early in order to get a seat that I prefer. The theatre is less than half filled. There are lots and lots of empty seats. A **multitude** of empty seats. There is, in fact, a **plethora** of empty seats. Sure enough, just as the lights dim, someone will come and park his or her keester in the seat immediately next to me, or directly in front of me.

Do people just have an innate need for security? Or am I just such a likable guy that I draw people to me?

Let me ask you this question. Don't worry, this is not a quiz. The waiting room at your doctor's office contains nine chairs. When you arrive two are occupied. Where would you sit? Would you sit immediately beside one of these two patients, or would you leave at least one chair space in between?

Don't get me wrong. I am not an anti-social person. But when there is a lot of space available, use it!

So the next time you find yourself in any of these situations, just take a moment to survey the surroundings to see if I am correct in my analysis. If you stop to do this, you will discover an important thing. You will discover that either these type of things do indeed happen to you on a regular basis, **or** that you yourself are the "Infringer"!

Are You a Survivor?

Are you surviving all of the Survivor Series that have appeared on television over the past few years? I haven't watched any of them. I refuse to get 'hooked' on watching them every week for a year, or however long they happen to run. I don't have the patience or the time to make such a commitment.

I've heard that there is a new one coming out shortly, however, the concept of which **does** appeals to me. And also, the series is more or less guaranteed not to last longer that a few episodes, if that.

Twenty contestants, both men and women, will be locked in a room that has no windows or pillows. Security cameras will constantly monitor them. Shortly after the contestants are locked in, Jazz will be piped into the room on a twenty-four hour basis. Any contestant can leave the room when he or she has had enough. (I figure this shouldn't take longer than a few hours). Suicide will be viewed as surrender. The Television Network and the sponsors of the program will not be held accountable for any murders that take place in the room, or any mental illness resulting from the severe mental strain. The families of any deceased members will get nothing. The last remaining survivor will walk away with one hundred, thousand dollars and probably little sanity.

One of the stipulations of the contest is that any black contestants participating must have their hands and feet bound to prevent them from dancing, as this would be unfair to the white folk.

Be sure to watch closely for this new series, because they are predicting it to be a short one!

The Second Coming of the Edsel

Believe it or not, there is a Pacer in my neighbourhood. You know, the little car that was on the market for four months in 1976. I don't remember who manufactured it. They are still trying to keep anonymous. I think it was either Ford or American Motors or maybe Gillespie Auto and Water Heater Makers.

For you younger folks who may have never seen a real "live" Pacer, it resembled a cone of silence on wheels. There was more glass than metal used in its construction. Because so much of the vehicle was transparent, the occupants enjoyed little in the way of privacy. Singing, scratching, picking, smoking, kissing, eating, etc. were all under full public observation when out on the road.

The Pacer, as this one in our neighbourhood testifies, can withstand the rigors of time, as long as it is not driven.

One of the selling features of the Pacer was that it could get thirty miles to the gallon. Now in the '70's this was **exceptional** performance. But what they *didn't* tell you was that the thirty miles to the gallon included the distance that it was pushed or towed which immediately brought that number down by fifty percent. I believe this has something to do with why it was named "Pacer". The owner would have to estimate how many times he or she would experience breakdown, to pace him or herself along the route to his or her destination. The manual for the vehicle included a formula that would aid the driver in calculating this, enabling him or her to make contingency plans in advance.

While putting the Pacer through the testing process at the testing facility, the test model apparently broke down on the way to the wall and required four men to push it the remaining distance to accomplish the crash. The testing facility was forced to design a new version of crash test dummies, as the ones normally used would not fit inside, and the dummies refused to travel in it no matter how short the trip.

Because of its small size, it could "turn on a dime", but seemed to have difficulty going forward. The structure of the front end caused it to be permanently out of alignment predisposing it to constantly veer toward every auto service station that came along.

I have seen this Pacer in antique car parades. It always follows a tow truck and has two guys behind pushing and another behind the wheel trying to keep it from veering into the crowd or any service station that happens to come along.

The Case of the Crooning Canary

The following is a true story...sort of...

Once upon a time a long, long time ago, when I was around ten years old, our neighbour family across the lane decided to move to Edmonton.

The day that they were to leave, they appeared on our back step to say good-bye. At the same time they asked if we would adopt their pet canary, as they didn't want to transport it on this long journey. My mother agreed, and "Dickie" became part of our family. Little did I know at the time that little Dickie was about to drive my brother and I insane with his infernal singing.

Dickie shared the bedroom with my brother and I, his cage hanging from a hook on the wall.

The remainder of the day following his arrival, Dickie was very quiet as he got accustomed to his new surroundings. At around midnight, my brother and I turned out the lights to go to sleep for the night. All was quiet for about three minutes, then out of the silence there suddenly emanated a

"trrrrrrrrrrrrrrrrrrreeeeeeeeeeeeeeepeepeepeep,
trrrrrrrrrrrrrrrrrrreeeeeeeeeeeeeeepeepeepeep."

We covered our heads with our pillows and put up with this racket for the rest of the night, but managed very little sleep.

After Dickie became acquainted with his surroundings he sang constantly, I mean non-stop, except when he slept, which was during the day when no one else was at home.

Needless to say that after a very short period of time by brother and I began to despise the little twerp. The only **good** thing that we saw in the whole situation was that our neighbour had told us that Dickie was twelve years old. We knew that a canary's life span was about ten to twelve years, therefore he would not be around too much longer.

Well Dickie lived and lived to spite us. At eighteen years old he was still going strong. While my brother and I were trying to study or do homework or talk on the phone in our bedroom, the little bundle of feathers would pipe up. Always quietly at first, feigning that he was tired or not feeling well, so that we would not remove him from our room and isolate him in the basement or kitchen. But sure enough, after a few minutes he would slowly begin to crescendo, until he had worked himself up into a full-blown bellowing frenzy,

**"TRRRRRRRRRRREEEEEEEEEEEPEEPEEP,
TRRRRRRRRRRREEEEEEEEEEEPEEPEEP."**

Man, my brother and I wanted to take the little pip-squeak outside and introduce him to the game of badminton!

Somewhere along the line, we discovered that Dickie hated the sound of paper being scrunched up. This sound really scared him. So guess what? Every time that he would pipe up we would scrunch up a piece of loose-leaf and throw it at his cage. This was usually good for about two or three minutes of silence. By the time we were finished our homework there would be pile of paper balls about four feet high under the cage.

On occasion when Dickie's trilling drove my brother and/or I over the edge, one of us would grab the handle on top of his cage and swing the cage above our head a few times pasting the little guy against the bars with the centrifugal force equal to a merry-go-round traveling at Mach 1. We think that he actually **enjoyed** this maneuver however. He would fall off of his perch and stagger about on the bottom of his cage for awhile, but then would shortly break into song once again, whereupon we would again provide him with another " ride of his life".

The Dickster was now approaching twenty. All of the feathers on his head had fallen out. He was bald. He looked like a miniature vulture. He became emaciated. He was losing his sight, but unfortunately his vocal chords remained vibrant.

My brother and I finally decided that it was time to take matters into our own hands. We began leaving Dickie's cage door open so that he could come out for "exercise". And he did too! He would come out and fly around the house bashing into walls and doors and sometimes people. He was as blind as a bat without radar. The picture window in the livingroom was his favorite target, and we always made sure that it was clean and polished and totally transparent. Come to think of it, we used to also leave the front door of the house open just in case Dickie got the urge to explore the great outdoors.

In the evening, after dark, when my brother and I would be watching TV in the livingroom, we would often hear Dickie flying from our bedroom down the hallway approaching the livingroom. We would quickly turn out all the lights and the TV and wait for Dickie to crash into something. We would then turn the lights back on and play "safari" as we competed to see which one of us could track him down and find him first. He was usually a little dazed, but that bird was as tough as nails. That's probably why he lived to be twenty-four years old!

When the day finally came, our Mother decided to bury Dickie in our backyard. Our whole family gathered for the solemn occasion to say good-bye to the little yella fella who had been a part of our family for some twelve years.

After planting him, my brother and I remained a bit longer than the others at the gravesite, to dedicate a little song to Dickie. It went something like this:

"trrrrrrrrrrrrrrrrrrrrrrrrreeeeeeeeeeeepeeepeeep, trrrrrrrrrrrrrrrrrrrrreeeeeeeeeepeeepeeep"

Don't You Just Hate It When...

Don't you just hate it when someone you've known for many years, like your spouse, doesn't like some of the food that you like, and refuses to let you eat it without feeling guilty?

"You're **not** going to put ketchup on those fried eggs, are you?"

"You're really **not** going to put ketchup on that steak!"

"I **forbid** you to put ketchup on that apple pie!"

"Get those pig's feet **out of my sight**!"

"If you eat that peanut butter and onion sandwich for your bedtime snack, you'll have to **sleep on the couch!** **IN YOUR PARENTS HOUSE!**"

"If you buy that jar of pickled herring, you are **not** bringing it into the house!"

I can't help it! I love pickled herring! My granddad loved pickled herring! My dad loved pickled herring! My brothers all love pickled herring! I can't help it, I love pickled herring! It's hereditary!

I usually buy a jar of pickled herring once a year. I then have to hide the jar in our shed in the backyard. When the "herring-hater" is busy on the phone or doing laundry, I sneak out to the shed and very quickly wolf down a couple of the little rascals.

Upon re-entering the house I must immediately either chew gum or gargle with ammonia so as not to give my secret away.

A lot of men have to sneak outside to have a smoke or a shot of liquor. I have to sneak outside to have a herring. I guess it would be worse if I had this affinity for <u>smoked </u>instead of pickled herring.

And what's wrong with pork sausages once in a while? On occasion I crave pork sausages. In my house this is akin to the cravings of a vice such as cigarettes, whiskey, or crack cocaine. When the cravings get intense enough that I have to surrender to them, I am forced to take a clandestine trip to the supermarket to purchase a package of the contraband, and then smuggle it into the house and bury it in the bottom of our freezer. When the opportune moment presents itself, that is when no one other than me is at home, I open all of the windows and doors (be it summer or winter), and quickly cook up the whole package of pink porkers. I then hide them in our refrigerator in the area that we reserve for spore development, to enjoy in a future moment of solitude.

One winter's evening my wife returned home unexpectedly while I was in the midst of cooking up a package of these pork delicacies. As she walked into the kitchen and spotted me skulking around the grease spitting frying pan in my parka, she did not utter a word as she raised both her hands in front of her, and crossed her index fingers as one would do when attempting to ward off a vampire.

On one occasion I took the family out to dinner. After our waitress asked me, "What kind of dressing would you like on your salad?" I sheepishly replied, "Blue cheese, please."
The reason I answer 'sheepishly' is because I never know what sort of reaction this response will elicit from my family. My wife and kids will often pinch their noses, cross their eyes, and give the thumbs down as a manner of their displeasure of my choice. This totally embarrasses me and often causes me to choose the soup.

Don't you just hate it when you listen to your voice mail at work upon your return from lunch, and hear a message in what sounds like a foreign language, the dialect of which you have never heard before, and the caller doesn't give you the name of his company, or what his account number is, but he **does** leave his name which sounds like 'Brnird Musgnofitz', so that you really can't call him back and ask for him by name, and he spurts out his long distance telephone number with his tongue moving faster than Pavorotti's in a Tim Horton's?

Don't you just hate it when you read in the TV Guide that there is an excellent movie on at

7:00 P.M. like "<u>The Mummy Returns</u>", and you rush to get all your work done and make popcorn and at 7:00 you turn on the TV only to find out that you were looking at Tuesday's movies and today is Wednesday, and the movie tonight is, "<u>Goober Returns to Mayberry</u>"?

Don't you just hate it when you are in the mall with a spouse or a friend and a perfect stranger comes up and says, "Hi Dennis, I haven't seen you for a long time! How are you doing? What are you doing these days? Do you still have that tattoo? Blah, blah, blah" and you have no idea who this person is?

You can't call them by name and you can't introduce them to the person that you're with. What are you supposed to say? "This is my wife Dawn. Dawn, I don't have a clue who the heck this person is!"

You really just want to escape from there as soon as possible so you say, "Well I really have to be going now. They have this huge sock sale on at Mal-Wart. It was nice to see you again. Say hi to the wife and kids, if you have any of either. Take care. Next time wear a name tag."

Don't you just hate it when you are thirty-four years old and a teen-ager on the bus calls you "sir" and offers you his seat?

Don't you just hate it when you're forty-five years old and a waitress offers you the senior's menu and tells you that the special of the day is minced ham, creamed cauliflower, mashed potatoes, and Jell-O?

Don't you just hate that?

You Know You're from a Small Town When...

You know you're from a small town when...

- You affectionately refer to the town's transit system as "our bus".
- The only ambulance driver moonlights as the only taxi cab driver.
- You can't wait to try on the new hip-waders that you got for Christmas.
- There are more people **in** the parade than there are watching it.
- The shot-putt event in a track and field meet involves a shotgun, a duck call, and a tourist.
- You have to special order furniture if you want any other colour than "camou-flage".
- A "night on the town" means circling overhead in your friend's pontooned Cessna.
- You describe the town's historic site as "a 1953 Dodge panel truck dispensing

French-fries.
- The hero of the town is a statue of a 50-foot carp, and you're proud of it!
- You plan your financial future around the casino.
- You install security lights on your house and garage and then leave them both unlocked.
- The local newspaper covers national and international events on the bottom corner of one page, but requires seven pages for sports coverage.
- Your idea of a traffic jam is ten cars waiting to pass a logging truck on the highway.
- The town's biggest celebrity is the guy who has hit more than five moose and deer with his pickup and is still alive to tell the tale
- You are noted as being a beautiful and kind person with a **terrific sense of humor!**

When Darkness Falls, So Do Its Victims

I guess most people are aware of the fact that we humans lose our sense of balance in the dark. I mean in <u>complete</u> darkness. If you didn't realize this, close your eyes and try untying and taking off your shoes while you are standing.

On occasion, my wife goes to bed before I do like last night for instance. When I came into the bedroom it was pitch black and I didn't want to awaken her. I was wearing sweatpants with elastic around the cuff. I kicked off my slippers. I then stood on one foot bending my other knee, and grabbed the cuff of my sweatpants. I pulled. No go. I lost my balance and had to put my foot down. I tried again. No go again. After the third or fourth attempt I was skipping around the bedroom like a newlywed. I began to get frustrated. The frustration turned into anger. I began to sweat. I began puffing like I had just run up three flights of stairs. I clenched my teeth and again stood on one foot. I bent my other knee. I grabbed the cuff of my sweatpants and yanked as hard as I could. I totally tangled myself up in my sweat-pants. I then completely lost my balance and fell backward onto the bed giving my wife a body slam. She woke up. She asked, "What are you doing?" I answered, "I'm getting undressed. Did I wake you?" I disengaged myself from my sweatpants and frantically rolled them into a ball and tossed them across the room. I then retired for the night.

Tips for Marital Bliss

FOR THE MEN:

Almost every married man will someday in his married life be asked these questions by his wife, "Do I look fat?" and "Do you still love me?"

The only correct and safe responses to these questions are "No, of course not!" and "Of course I do!" A hasty departure from the room is then strongly recommended. If you are in bed at the time one or (heaven forbid) both of these perilous questions arise, use the applicable response(s) suggested above, and then immediately begin to fake snoring, or go to the kitchen to make yourself a ham sandwich.

Following are some of the responses that non-thinking males have blurted out in the past which have greatly damaged their marital relationships and their skulls. These types of responses should be avoided at all times no matter how honest and truthful they may be:

Question: "Honey, do I look fat?"

Wrong responses:

a) "Compared to what?"

b) "I wouldn't call you fat, but I wouldn't call you thin either."

c) "That little extra weight looks good on you."

d) "I've seen fatter."

e) "Could you repeat the question? I was concentrating on your insurance policy here."

f) "Why do you ask? Is it because of that little incident last week when you were standing on a street corner downtown and a cop came up to you and said, "OK, break it up!"

Question: "Honey, do you still love me?"

Wrong responses:

a) "I suppose so."

b) "Would it make you feel better if I say 'Yes'?"

c) "That depends on what you mean by 'Love'."

d) "Does it matter?"

e) "Who, me?"

f) "Shhhhh, Don Cherry's on."

g) "I'm still here ain't I?"

Any of these wrong responses given on the spur of the moment, in a nano second of inadvertent loss of sanity, will cost you big time. Usually a card, dinner, flowers, and silence will follow comatose responses like these, let alone several sleepless nights alone on the couch.

Remember guys, always be on your toes for these short snappers that come out of left field when you least expect it. Don't be caught off guard!

FOR THE WOMEN:

Most warm-blooded males have difficulty in understanding the phrase "I have a headache" when delivered by their wives.

I searched for the definition in <u>Bud's Totally Abridged Dictionary</u>, which defines 'headache' as, "A nerve pain in the head".

Ladies, my tip to you regarding this is to **never** use this destructive phrase **past the hour of 8:00 PM**. To men, this statement carries a totally different meaning before 8:00 PM than it does after. If the mood is not conducive, please just state that fact. "I have a headache" carries such negative connotations and is used so often on TV and in the general public as a comical idiom, that it means absolutely nothing to the average warm-blooded serious male.

Hearing this dastardly phrase past the hour of **10:30 PM** brings about an immediate feeling of rejection in the male, and may do permanent damage to the relationship.

So ladies, try never to use the phrase "I have a headache" past the hour of 8:00 PM.

Another approach that will definitely not work, is for you to state the following to your husband at **5:00 PM**, "I **will be** having a headache at around 11:00 PM tonight".

Following are a few other words or phrases that you ladies should try to avoid if at all possible in order to keep your marriage on firm ground:

a) "I'm too tired".
b) "It's too late".
c) "I'm not feeling well."
d) "No!"
e) "Tomorrow!"
f) "Not here!"
g) "The kids will hear!"
h) "The guests will hear!"
i) "It's not our anniversary!"
j) "Doesn't this morning count?"
k) "Again?"
l) "Take a shower!"
m) "Can't we just read?"
m) "My nurse is due back any minute!"

So ladies, if you avoid these phrases at all times I guarantee you many happy and blissful years of marriage.

To Eat or Not To Eat

Isn't it funny how the eggheads in the medical profession have suddenly changed their tune concerning the nutritional value of some of the foods we eat?

In my younger days these bigwigs denounced the consumption of certain foods and drink and promoted the consumption of others. But they have now done an about face and are now pontificating the opposite.

We are all *now* well aware of the excellent medicinal attributes of wine. Yes folks, drink at least one glass of wine per day and this will stimulate your heart and aid in your digestive and circulation systems. In my day, any consumption of any alcohol was strictly frowned upon, unless of course you were a priest.

We are *now* being told that chocolate is good for us. If chocolate is good for us that means by juxtaposition, ipso fatso, that caffeine must be good for us also since chocolate is laced with caffeine. It stimulates the heart; speeds up the circulation. So bring on the coffee, tea, expressos, and let me drown in lattes.

We also *now* have been made aware of the tremendous health benefits of aspirin. Years ago we were told that eating too much of this stuff would damage the lining of our stomachs and cause ulcers. Now we are told that we should take one per day instead of an apple to keep the doctor away. (Which is not difficult to do in this day and age where a "house call" to a doctor means a call on his cell phone from the golf course to his house).

I have **now** just recently heard that hot dogs are good for us. Apparently all of the junk that you find in wieners is so vile that once digested it will help build up our immune system to help ward off leprosy.

On the other hand, medical scientists are telling us that the stuff that they told us years ago that **was** good for us is now **not good** for us.

Carrots and turnips are **now** a no-no. Although they promote keener eyesight, it has been recently discovered that they can shorten your life. Eating a lot of this junk will enable you to very clearly see the faces of all your family and friends as they surround your death- bed.

And what about the myth of milk? When I was a kid I was forced to drink a cubic gallon of this stuff every day. All that calcium would ensure that I would have strong and healthy bones for the rest of my life.

Now all the lactic acid and fat in the milk can cause you to have a stroke and die at an early age. So where does that leave us? Well, a thousand years from now some Anthropologist will uncover us and make the following determination: "My but these bones and teeth are in excellent condition! This person must have drunk at least a cubic gallon of milk everyday of his life. It also appears as if this person was about thirty-two years old when he died".

So let's **now** all follow the example of the inhabitants of Mongolia who are noted for their longevity, and replace that glass of milk with a liter of wine. Consume at least one hot dog per day followed by an aspirin. Snack on chocolate throughout the day and don't miss any coffee breaks for that extra jolt of caffeine. And for goodness sake, stay away from those tubers and veggies!

I know what I'll be snacking on tonight while watching the hockey game!

P.s. Potato chips...friend or foe?

The Key Element

Why, in classical music do they always tell you in which key the piece is written?

"Minuet in G", "Beethoven's 18th symphony in F minor".

Who the heck cares?

Did the composers really think that without supplying this crucial information some listener would say, "Gee, that's a great piece! I wonder what key it's in." Or were they anticipating that a symphony patron might one evening be comfortably seated in a concert hall enjoying the performance whereupon he would realize that it is too dark to read the program. He immediately begins to wonder to himself, "Gee, I wonder what the heck key they are playing this piece in?" Out of desperation he wakes up the guy seated beside him and asks, "Hey Bub, do you have any idea what key they're in?"

They don't do this in contemporary music. You never hear of song titles such as, Elton John's "Rocket Man in the key of E".

Who the heck cares?

It could be in the key of H# for all I care. Most people in the audience wouldn't know a key signature from a question mark anyway!

Did the composers think that some people might not listen to a particular piece of music if it was written in a key that they didn't care for?

Radio announcer: "And now for your listening pleasure, here is Mendelson's 'Dancing in the Barnyard' in the key of B# major."
Listener: "Aw gee, not B# major! I hate that key! Quick, switch the station! I'm not going to listen to that!"

My thinking on this subject is that these composers were just trying to impress people...

"Wow, Bach composed this piece in the key of G#major7-5. It would have been so much easier to write it in the key of C. Wow, he da man!"

Maybe the composers just took pleasure in watching the musicians in the orchestra sweat as they struggled to play in these impossible keys...

French horn player: "If I ever bump into the composer who wrote this piece of music in this key, I'll fix it so that he'll be able to play a French horn duet, *solo!*"

Did these symphonic pieces not have "real" titles because most of them had no lyrics? No theme? They were just a bunch of notes put on paper and upon completion the composer would scan the score and say to himself, "What the heck am I going to call this mess of notes? Let's see...how about 'Dusk at the Anthill', or maybe 'Rose, Thy Name is Smelly', or how about 'I'm Just a Parrotless Pirate in Love'. I just really can't decide. Well let's see, it **was** written in the key of Fminor9 sus. Hey, that's kind of a catchy title! Maybe I should just go with that!"

And so it went.

Did You Ever Have One of Those Days?

Did you ever have one of those days when you get up in the morning to go to work and you're just in a daze? You feel dizzy and your mind can't focus? You stand in front of your closet for ten minutes staring at the eighteen shirts you have hanging in there but you can't make a decision which one to wear? You go to the bathroom and struggle for two minutes before you discover that your underwear is on backwards? The top of your deodorant breaks off and falls into the sink? You drop a spoon on the kitchen floor and you stoop over four times to pick it up missing it on the first three attempts? You go to make your lunch and find there is only one slice of bread left, and it's moldy? You go to pour your tea and hot water comes out of the teapot because you forgot to put in a tea bag? You put on your shoes and discover the knot you left in your laces the night before because you were too fatigued to undo it? You zip up your coat and the zipper goes over the lining and becomes so jammed that you can't zip it up or down and now you find yourself in a self-imposed straight jacket?

You go out to start your car because it's forty below zero outside and discover that you forgot to plug it in last night? You get every red light possible on the way to work and every car has a woman driver in it? As you pull into the parking lot at work you remember with fondness the keys to your office that you left by the front door of your house? You finally sit down at your desk with your coat on that you can't get out of and notice your red message light flashing on your phone and you listen to the perfunctory message that tells you that you have sixteen messages from 5:05 p.m. yesterday? You fire up your computer and begin to think up unkind words because you think that it's frozen because the cursor won't move but then you discover that you've been sliding your stapler around the top of your desk instead of your mouse? Your boss then walks in and asks how you are and you lie and say that you feel great and he answers, "Good, because I need you to work late tonight"? And you begin to get stomach cramps from the Noodles Alfredo and grape Kool-Aid you had before going to bed last night just as a headache begins to kick in? Your assistant then calls to tell you that she won't be coming in today because she won ten thousand dollars at the casino last night and stayed up until four o'clock in the morning celebrating? Then an overly cheerful staff member comes up to you and reminds you of the staff meeting about to take place in twenty minutes at which you are scheduled to give a presentation to which you reply, "Is that today?" At lunchtime you open your lunch only to find that you have tomato sandwiches for the fourteenth time this month and get furious that your wife can't be more creative and caring, but then you remember that you're not married and that you make your own lunches? You drag yourself into your house at eleven o'clock P.M. and your dog bites you because he's not used to you coming home after dark? You sit down on the sofa with your T.V. dinner to watch "The Mummy" that you set your VCR to tape earlier in the evening, but instead the movie you actually taped is "Pee Wee Herman Meets the Hell's Angels" because you thought today was Wednesday but it's actually Thursday and "The Mummy" was on yesterday? Just as you decide to give it up and go to bed, you remember that Thursday is your shopping night and you have no food in the house except for a few tomatoes and a piece of moldy bread?

Did you ever have one of those days?

King or Queen of the Throne

Although I am not a big advocate of Women's Lib, I believe that women have made their bed and now they must lie in it on this issue.

The toilet seat controversy has existed since xxxx when John Crapper invented the flush toilet. (I am **not** kidding! Look it up!) This may not be a huge problem for newlyweds as they are willing to put up with the idiosyncrasies of their new spouses, but as time wears on so do the nerves.

This appears to be a problem for females only, as I never hear of males complaining about their wives or daughters not **putting the seat up.** I personally feel that the males are showing consideration by leaving the seat up. What they are actually saying by doing this is "I am leaving the seat up to show you that I **did indeed** raise the seat, therefore not leaving a mess for you to sit on or clean up after me." Very few women seem to recognize this grand gesture as being an act of love.

But failing all else, if this remains a contentious issue in your marriage, there *are* solutions available. Here are my suggestions for the porcelain problem:

1) both male and female put **both** the lid and the seat down so that the same amount of effort is required by each, **or**

2) the males put the seat down **and** the females put the seat up when done, **or**

3) the status quo is maintained **and** the females stop complaining, **or**

4) if you have more than one bathroom, one belongs to each party and they can do whatever they want when in their own territory, but must respect the rules of the other when on foreign tile, **or**

5) "the majority rules" as in some households where there may be one female and four males, the seat would remain up at all times.

Speaking on a personal note, my wife never complains about toilet seat positioning. #5 above applies to our family. She has even "taken the plunge" in the wee hours of the morning when half asleep and in the dark.

In summary, I feel that all females must really think carefully about their toilet seat trials, and search for equity rather than try to yoke all males with their problem. Once they have done this, they will soon and unequivocally realize that they cannot just continue to roll through life without ever having to put a toilet seat up. Let's face it, if there were no men in the world, or if our equipment were different, there would be no hinges on toilet seats.

The late Mr. Crapper would turn in his grave if he knew the controversy that has been created over his magnificent invention.

There is no **one** solution to the "seat saga" but there **are** several alternatives! Amen.

Half Full or Half Empty

I have never quite understood the analogy of "is the glass half full or half empty".

I fully understand what it is <u>supposed</u> to question, that being:
   a) do you **actually know** if the glass is half full or half empty
   b) if you don't **actually** know, and you view it as being half full you are an optimist,
   or,
   if you view it as being half empty you are a pessimist.

I don't agree with any of this!

If you are the one pouring the water into or out of the glass, or you are present to witness the pouring of the water into or out of the glass, then you <u>actually</u> know if the glass is half full or half empty. If the glass is in the process of being filled, then it is half full when it has been half filled. If the glass is in the process of being emptied, then it is half-empty when it has been half emptied. Something cannot be half-empty if it was never full! There is no question about this!

If you are <u>not</u> present, but just walk into a

room with a half a glass of water sitting on a table, and you are asked the question, "Is that glass half full or half empty", I believe that I would be an **optimist** if I responded, "It is half empty", and a **pessimist** if I answered "It is half full".

Why? What is my logic?

Because if the glass was filled, i.e. to the top, and then half was removed, that would mean either one of two things:

a) someone was thirsty and drank half of the water from the glass,

b) you are living in a country where you can afford to spill out half of a glass of water just to prove this ridiculous point.

These are two positive points:

a) someone was thirsty but now they are not

b) you don't live in Afghanistan

Now, if you respond that the glass is half full, I believe that you would be pessimistic because if the glass is half full, it would mean one of two things:

a) someone is thirsty but has not yet had a drink because the glass has not yet been filled

b) the glass was never filled so no water has been dumped out

These are two negative points:

a) the person is still thirsty and has not yet

had a drink
b) you are probably living in Afghanistan

So my theory debunks the commonly held theory completely!

The next time someone asks you, "Is the glass half full or half empty?" simply and proudly answer, "It's half empty of course! I am an eternal optimist, don't you know! And I don't live in Afghanistan!" Then watch the expression on their face!

Handy Man Special

Let me begin by saying that I am **not** making any of the following up. Let me also say that this is **not** a recreation of a "3 Stooges" comedy short. What I am about to relate is absolutely one hundred per cent unadulterated truth. I have had to change the names of the characters involved because of my close relationship to them, and because of my generous nature, so as to save them from embarrassment.

This whole escapade began when my brother "Curly", decided to insulate and drywall the unfinished basement of his house. His retired father-in-law, "Larry", immediately offered his assistance to the project looking forward to spending some of his abundant free time with his son-in-law, Curly.

After all the building supplies were ordered and delivered, they were ready to begin. Curly began by measuring and cutting some of the lumber using a handsaw, while Larry began nailing together the framework for the first wall. On one of the backswings of the hammer, the head suddenly detached from the handle and flew some four feet catching Curly beneath his left eye. Besides being quite startled, Curly only sustained minor injuries, as the skin beneath the eye was not cut open. There was considerable swelling however, and the pigment around the eye quickly changed from pink to red to purple within minutes.

After apologies were made and a new hammer was employed, the twosome decided to switch tasks with Larry now working the handsaw and Curly doing his best to hammer the framework together using his one good eye. A short time later a sharp cry of pain emanated from the basement. The saw had slipped in Larry's hand on a forward stroke causing Larry to inflict a massive gash in his left hand. In fact, he almost dismembered his thumb as the cut ran between his thumb and index finger. Bandaging the wound up as best they could, Curly then drove Larry to the hospital where he received a tetanus shot, stitches, and fresh bandaging.

While returning from the hospital, Curly suggested that Larry call it a day and go home to rest. But Larry would have none of that. "Nah, it's just a flesh wound", he retorted.

Back in the basement, Curly with his swollen black eye and Larry with his left thumb heavily bandaged, the dynamic duo got right back to business. Curly once again switched from hammering and took the saw away from Larry before anymore damage could be done. He then suggested that Larry work on something a little less dangerous than hammering or sawing.

Larry agreed and began using the power drill to drill screws into the framework and then into the basement floor.

All went smoothly for the next few minutes when all of a sudden above the noise of the sawing and drilling, Curly heard the calm but amazed voice of Larry say, "Well, would you look at that!"

Curly was working with his back to Larry at this point, so as he turned his head to look at Larry through his one good eye, he witnessed Larry standing upright holding up in front of himself both the drill and his injured thumb. While holding a screw in place with his left thumb and index finger and then attempting to screw it down with the drill, a loose thread from the bandage had become entwined on the drill bit. Because of the extremely rapid spinning of the bit, before Larry could react, half of the bandage had been transferred from his thumb to the drill bit. Now this normally would have been quite a humorous incident, but taking into account all that had preceded it, only an awed silence filled the basement.

It was at this point that the mutual decision was made that it would be the wiser and safer thing to do if the project was put on hold for an indefinite period of time to provide opportunity for recuperation.

When Mrs. Curly pulled her car into the driveway and stepped out, she was shocked to find a trail of blood leading to the front door and a discarded hammerhead lying on the front lawn. Upon entering the house in an agitated state, she found her father Larry, and her husband Curly, lounging in the family room watching television and drinking coffee. Before an explanation could be offered, Mrs. Curly noticed in shock her husband's swollen black eye and her father's half-bandaged hand. Without looking up to acknowledge her presence, the two defeated handymen continued to stare at the figure skating they were watching on the television as Curly muttered," Don't even ask!"

A Taxing Proposition
(How to Keep Your Assets Liquid)

I will be attending a seminar next month that I am not at all looking forward to. The subject matter will be dealing with the implication, ramification, and constipation of our federal tax laws as they relate to the small to medium businesses in our communities.

The main thrust of the seminar will be to come up with viable solutions to aid in keeping these smaller businesses functioning smoothly and regularly.

The two guest speakers, L.K.Seltzer, and Randy Backhouse, are reported to be extremely fluid in their respective presentations.

Randy will be addressing the mess being made by the Feds, while Leonard will dwell on the sluggishness of the economy, and also on the steps we can all take to promote a more rapid release of binding governmental constrictions.

This will be an exceptionally difficult seminar for me to stomach as I have very strong and emotional feelings concerning the direction the Government has taken which has been cramping the small business man in our country for decades.

Hopefully with the introduction of some outside assistance, a purging of old school mentality will take place and open the door for new and solid growth.

Horsestuff

Have you ever wondered where and how some of our unusual words and sayings originated? Well today's your lucky day!

I will attempt to enlighten you on the origins of the word "Horseradish"and the saying "Straight from the horse's mouth".

Horseradish is made from the pungent root of the horseradish plant which is cultivated to make this condiment used on roast beef, or mixed with beets in various degrees to make mild, strong, or "hoo boy, that's hot!" horseradish. So, the root resembles that of the radish, which is also a strong, sharp tasting vegetable.

Now we all know that the horse is a very powerful creature and lends its name to such powerful or loud things as Horsepower, Horsefly, Horseplay, Horselaugh, and Horsemanure.

As the story goes, in England where they eat a considerable amount of roast beef, in the year 1753, one Murray Statham was feeding carrots to the two horses that were hitched up to his wagon. He was in town about to pick up his weekly supplies. By mistake, some of the radish roots from his garden got mixed in with his carrots. He fed them to his horses. Nostrils flared. Eyes watered and then bugged out.

Hooves stomped. Finally the team took off. Murray was still positioned in front of the team still trying to force feed the beasts. They trampled him. The wagon ran over him. He was dragged through the streets of the town for half an hour until the effects of the radish roots on the horses wore off.

All of the town folk talked about this episode for weeks afterwards. There were many horselaughs heard in the local tavern.

From that day forward the powerful radish root that caused Murray Statham's horses to lose their senses has been known as "Horseradish".

The popular saying "I heard that 'straight from the horse's mouth'" goes back to the Mongols circa 900 AD.

The horse was a very prized and valuable commodity to the Mongols, especially during times of war, which for the Mongols, was everyday.

Although these horses were very powerful and faithful to their owners, they also possessed extremely bad breath. If you were able to stand in front of your horse while it breathed on you without passing out, you were considered to be a noble and brave warrior.

Therefore, if you reported something "Straight from the horse's mouth", that would mean in personified terms that you had the stamina and the stomach to stand before your horse and have him tell you to your face the news that you are relating. If you were brave and strong enough to accomplish this, then you must be a brave and noble individual. Therefore the news that you are imparting would always be considered truthful.

Now **you** have it **"Straight from the horse's mouth!"**

The Hecks Angels

There are many cities in Canada that are currently experiencing endemic problems with street gangs. The "Hell's Angels" have moved into a number of the larger cities, and less infamous, but just as disturbing local gangs are rising up across the country.

It appears that even the small town communities are now encompassing similar societal problems, and because of the lack of sufficient law enforcement, are becoming increasingly and justifiably concerned.

Recently I happened to read the local newspaper of one such small town located in the south of Saskatchewan. I could not believe the front-page story! I will briefly detail the important elements of the event.

The headline read,

"Gang Terrorizes Community".

The accompanying photos were graphic and ugly.

It appears that a local gang has risen from this small community of two hundred and sixty-two in population. They have announced themselves as "The Heck's Angels".

Over the weekend in question, members of

this gang rode up and down, around and through this tiny community on their mountain bikes screaming obscenities such as, **"You Stink!"** and **"Your mother wears running shoes!"** at innocent bystanders.

The trouble escalated after dark. A drive-by egging was reported on the corner of First Street and First Street, where inhabitant Samuel Whilms and his family reluctantly became a six-egg omelet.

"They peddled by so fast all's I could make out was the insignias on the backs of their black flannel jackets", Mr. Whilms was reported as saying immediately following the attack. The insignia was a skull and slingshot.

The gang then accosted two teenage males, threatening them to either hand over their suspenders or suffer the consequences.

The two youths did manage to get a good look at their assailants as they de-suspender-ized themselves. All six members of the gang were described as being five feet ten inches tall, approximately one hundred and sixty pounds, well tanned with dark hair and beards, black leather shoes, black pants, black flannel jackets, black hats, and black suspenders.

Buggies were overturned. Two horses were taken for joy rides and were found later the next day all sweaty and full of burrs. One of the gang members even had the audacity to paint an "angry face" on one of the horse's haunches with yellow paint.

Other graffiti found around the community the following morning included, "Go to heck!" sprawled across the Mill's barn, and "Brother Ebineezer smells like chicken droppings!" was wrapped around the Abramson's silo.

It is also believed that gang members are pushing illegal substances to the youth in the community. Adults have found bubble gum and chocolate bar wrappers in the playgrounds. Empty lipstick and other cosmetic containers have also been seen along the roadside. One mother found a "Mad Magazine" in her teenage son's bedroom hidden under the mattress. A yellow kerchief found in a dresser drawer amongst her nine black ones, was enough to get a young girl into hot water with her parents.

The elders of the town are totally stunned at these occurrences and are beside themselves at coming up with any sort of solution.

No one knows the identity of the guilty scoundrels and until they slip up and get caught, few of the town's inhabitants will be getting a restful night's sleep.

Gee, Thanks a Lot!

Have you ever had this happen to you?

One Saturday morning I was standing in line at a cashier waiting patiently, as I always do, to pay for my purchase at a large tire store that is Canadian owned. (The name of the store need not be identified).

I was purchasing a wheelbarrow. It was in a box, and was quite heavy and awkward to deal with.

As I was slowly shuffling along sliding the large box in front of me, smiling and thinking to myself about all the work that I had waiting for me at home, a voice coming from directly behind me out of the clear blue sky said to me, "They have that exact same wheelbarrow at Mal-Wart (not the real name), on special for twenty-five dollars less."

Now why would this complete stranger offer this information to me? Was it because...

   a) He is actually a nice guy and wants to save me some money? (not likely)
   b) He wants me to go to Mal-Wart (ficti-tious name) so that he can get my

place in line? (very highly likely)

c) He is a mean person who is trying to embarrass me in front of several other customers by pointing out that I am getting ripped off, and that he got a much better deal because he is more intelligent than me? (could be)

d) He is just one of "those kinds of people" who loves to talk and has to be talking whenever he is awake?
(These people always seek me out in public places.)
(happens all the time)

e) He is the owner of Mal-Wart (bogus name), and is just trying to get me to go and buy my wheelbarrow over there.
(stranger things have happened)

I fell for this ruse only once before, before I learned my lesson. In that particular instance, I did in fact leave my place in line. I then dragged the wheelbarrow, or whatever it was, back to the aisle I took it from, and went to Mal-Wart (not the real name), in order to save myself the twenty-five bucks.

BUT, once I got to Mal-Wart (fake name)...

a) I couldn't find the "special" wheelbarrows.

b) I couldn't find a salesclerk.

c) I couldn't find the manager. (I think he was in the store that I had just left.)

d) There were only five wheelbarrows that

ever were on sale,

e) These wheelbarrows were advertised in a flyer two months ago.

f) All that they had left in their wheelbarrow inventory were either larger or smaller than the size that I wanted.

So needless to say, I had to return to the Canadian owned tire store to get the wheelbarrow that I wanted.

Since that experience, whenever some guy in a cashier's line tells me that I can get a better deal at another store for what I am about to buy, I ask him, "Why are you telling me this?" Then I proceed to list off the possible reasons A to E as listed above. Then I proudly tell him that I only paid $1.98 for the windshield washer fluid at Sellarz (another made up name), as I point to the jug of the stuff that he is holding in his left hand that has a $2.29 price sticker on it. I then tell him that *__I already know__* about this special at the other store, but *__I want to pay more__* so that I can earn more points, and that he should mind his own business.

So memorize this valuable information so that the next time some busybody tries to embarrass you in a checkout line, you will be well prepared to deal with him.

Don't Blame Fido

Do you know one thing that I have never been able to understand? Why when we were all in school, there were always several kids who would blame their dogs for eating their homework. And the funny thing was that the teachers always fell for it!

Teacher: "Ralphie, where is you homework!"

Ralphie: "My dog ate it, Mrs. Ogilvie."

Teacher: "OK, you can just take a nap while the rest of the class goes over the assignment."

I mean, the teachers never even asked any questions. If I was a teacher, God forbid, and some kid laid this one on me, I'd ask what the dog's name was. That alone would stump half of the kids right there because they didn't have a dog in the first place!

Next, I would ask if their dog had an appetite for loose-leaf, since this was the third time this week the mutt has dined on English Literature.

Then I would ask if the pulp-loving pup cared for any other kinds of paper products such as the daily newspaper, hockey cards, wallpaper, or toilet paper, or whether it was just the written word that sparked its appetite.

Maybe the dog was literate, and just thought that the assignment was so crappy, that it decided to destroy it the only way it knew how, by ingesting it.

I myself never tried this ruse. I guess that I was just too honest a kid and just couldn't tell a lie. Not that we didn't have a dog at home. We did have a dog in the house, Buddie. But he didn't care much for the taste of Hilroy. Even when I would smear bacon drippings over my notebooks, he still refused to rip them to shreds. He would sniff around and lick at the bacon grease, but he just would not eat my homework.

Once our canary ate my homework though, and when I reported this to my teacher the next morning, I received a detention for after school.

On another occasion, I was doing my homework at a friend's place when his cat decided to use my scribbler for a litterbox. The next morning I went to school without my homework and was sent to the principal's office for telling the truth.

I don't know what it was about the "dog story", but it always seemed to work. Maybe the secret is to get your dog at a very early age and begin training it immediately to eat homework. I recommend that this be done over the summer holidays, so that by fall your dog will have developed a taste for print. Maybe it is because most everyone loves dogs and are therefore willing to accept the little mischievous things that dogs do, like eating homework, eating your shoes, eating your couch, or eating your next door neighbour.

If you have any friends or family who happen to be teachers, please inform them that the excuse "Fido ate my homework" is most probably a big fat fib, and they shouldn't fall for it.

And one more thing, canaries make great paper shredders!

Christmas Cheer?

Is there anyone who doesn't enjoy Christmas and all the many things associated with it? Well if there is "Bah humbug to them!"

Once the Christmas spirit gets hold of me there's little that can stop me. I know because several individuals have tried.

Take my wife for example. One evening a few weeks before the big day I decided to help her by doing some Yuletide activities. I first wrapped all the gifts that we had purchased thus far. I decided to do this on the bed in our bedroom so that I could close the door and have the necessary privacy required (with three snoopy sons and wife roaming around). This is something I would not recommend however unless you take some necessary precautions which I obviously overlooked.

After cutting the wrapping paper for an exceptionally large gift I noticed that I had inadvertently cut through the bedspread. We own a queen-sized bed but we now have twin bedspreads to cover it.

I next decided to help my wife in the kitchen. She was making rum balls. This is a very tedious job. You have to roll the mixture into balls and then roll the balls in icing sugar to coat them.

I love these things, so I began making the balls a good hefty size, about the size of a snowball. My plan was that I could get through the huge bowl of mixture quite quickly if I only had to make a dozen balls.

Whilst I was in the process of rolling out the ninth ball my wife happened to come by. After a quick glance she wailed, "Those are **way** too big!" and proceeded to show me the "correct" size to make them to which I replied, "You've got to be kidding! It will take me two days to roll this mixture into balls that size!" I then continued, "And besides, we all love rum balls! Why not make big portions so that I only have to eat one or two rather than twelve at a time!" But noooooo. You see they have to look *dainty* on the dessert tray. To which I responded, "OK, I'll make a few *dainty* ones and then a few humungus ones for us pig-type people." She didn't care for this suggestion.

So after four hours of backbreaking labour, I was finally done. At this point I was sick of rum balls, not because I had just made two hundred and forty-three of them but because I had eaten half of the mixture. If I hadn't eaten half of the mixture I estimate I would have had to make five hundred of the suckers.

While I was enjoying this task, my wife was making mincemeat tarts. Now I **_love_** mincemeat! I looked at the piddly tarts she was baking and asked, "why not make bigger tarts so that I can at least taste the mincemeat rather than just the pastry?"

"No, they have to look **dainty**"she replied. There was that word again!

"So make me a mincemeat **pie** then, and I'll eat it in the backyard by myself so no one will be witness to my 'undaintiness'," I replied.

When she unintentionally and regrettably mentioned to me that she would be making shortbread cookies the next evening, I once again volunteered my assistance. When I reported for duty and presented a Frisbee as my cookie-cutter, she recommended that I go and shovel snow.

You see **dainty** isn't in a man's vocabulary. If a man likes something, if it tastes good to him, he will just keep on eating it until it is either gone or he doesn't want anymore. They don't serve **dainties** at a bachelor party or at a Grey Cup party. We men will just fill our faces until we're stuffed, or maybe even until we're sick. End of story. What could be simpler? How else could you tell when you've had enough?

How Much is That Doggie on the Menu

In the recent past, the World Cup Soccer (Football, if you are not North American) matches were held in Korea and Japan.

There was a considerable amount of controversy stirred up by many of the foreigners who visited these two countries to witness the games. The controversy did not surround the football matches themselves, but was directed at some of the food that the foreigners discovered being served in many of the local restaurants.

Apparently, one of the main dishes of these countries is dog. They have dog on almost all of the restaurant menus, and there are some establishments that serve nothing but. (These latter establishments are called "Dog Houses").

Most Westerners had a real problem with this. I personally didn't see any problem. My thinking was that if they didn't want it, they didn't have to eat it. This is a part of Oriental culture. They eat all kinds of weird things over there like raw fish, live baby octopus, squid, sea horses, snake, insects, eggplant, and Big Macs with side orders of rice instead of fries. I can't understand why the foreigners were complaining without even trying any of these dishes.

I believe that this practice is very proactive, that is, by means of getting all of those roaming, stray dogs off of the streets. The Humane Society kennels are virtually empty on a consistent basis, and are appropriately called "Marketplaces" by the local restaurateurs.

If I ever had the opportunity to visit over there, I would take a shot at tasting some of their canine cuisine, for instance:

- Hot dogs (literal)
- Baby puppy ribs
- Canine stew
- Fido fricassee
- (German) Shepherd Pie
- Stuffed bowser
- Lassie loaf
- Pekinese chops
- Casserole a la Spaniel
- Schnauzer on a stick
- Bulldog burgers
- Barbecued Sheepdog with Creole sauce
- Husky hash
- Pit Bull pie
- Shitzu shish-ka-bob
- Mutt's tail
- Boiled Whippet – for the weight watchers
- Smoked St. Bernard – the hungry man's special

Due to the tremendous number of visitors during these games, in order to accommodate them in restaurants as far as reading and ordering from the menus, the menus contained coloured pictures of a variety of hounds that were presently being served in the respective establishments. Also, each picture was numbered. So if the picture of the imported Irish Setter happened to catch your eye, all that was required was to write down #5 on the piece of paper supplied by your waiter or waitress. If, on the other hand, the Doberman looked particularly appetizing, you would simply jot down #13. Combos were also available which made dining in groups of four or more much more fun and exciting.

Now I would think that when ordering any of these dishes, a certain amount of diplomacy should be utilized. For example:

- Don't whistle and yell "Here girl"at your waitress when ready to order
- Don't command her to "go fetch" your food
- Don't act surprised if your food is served in a bowl with your name on it
- Try not to shed or drool on the tablecloth
- When leaving, try to just say thank you to your waitress without patting her on the head
- And for goodness sake, **do not** under any circumstances ask for a **Doggie Bag!**

When back out on the street, if a sudden urge should arise to chase down a moving vehicle, it should be remembered that this is perfectly normal and the urge should subside within the hour. (Or much faster if one does not control the urge and actually does engage in some serious street sprinting).

The good news is that there is little danger involved, as most of the cars are of the small variety and therefore can't do much damage to any tourist that they happen to run over. The majority of the vehicular traffic on the streets remains to be bicycles and scooters, which are very easy to run down without much effort or threat of injury.

And as far as the inhabitants of the cities are concerned, they would much rather have these tinhorn tourists chasing cars and bicycles in their streets than to find them taking care of other business in their parks!

What's Next?

A couple of weeks before Christmas, I was in a shopping mall minding my own business, when suddenly I heard dogs barking.

My first thought was that maybe one of those demonstrations was being held in the Centre Court that features dogs that perform all kinds of amazing tricks.

Working my way through the crowds of shoppers in an effort to arrive at the site of the performance before it was over, I finally reached the Centre Court when...

"What to my wondering eyes should appear,
    But children **and dogs** in line to have pictures taken
    sitting on Santa's knee."

Yes folks, jolly ol' St. Nick has gone to the dogs! Now there is Sally, and Billy and Johnny and Fido too!

Why does the shopping mall allow this? It's bad enough standing in line just to get your kid to sit on Santa's knee and get his or her picture taken with the furry fellow. But now the lineups are longer because there are dogs in it! What if a dog bites a little kid while standing in line? What if a dog lifts its leg on Santa?

I have a plan to end all of this nonsense. My wife owns a killer parrot. I am going to bring "Baby" (a misnomer if there ever was one) to the mall to have its picture taken with Santa. How can they refuse me now? The precedent has been set! If a kid in line happens to ask me, "Can I pet your parrot?" I'll answer, "Sure, if you don't mind being called Stumpy the rest of your life!"

Baby will first scream louder and shriller than any dog can bark. Then she will terrorize all the children and adults that are standing in the line. When we finally get to Santa to have her picture taken, she will rip Santa's suit to shreds in Tasmanian Devil-like style in a whirlwind of beaks, claws and red and white velvet.

This episode will probably make the newspaper with headlines something like:

"Parrot Terrorizes Mall – Evacuation Causes Stampede"

"Santa and Elves in Shock – Santa vows to 'Hang up his beard'"

"Children Traumatized by Perilous Parrot"

"Swat Team and Animal Services Called In"

Well there you have it, yet another exploitation of Christmas. Maybe some other kids will catch on and bring **their** pets to the mall to get **their** pictures taken with Santa. Gerbils, ferrets, goldfish.......What's next?

The Christmas List

Do you suffer from that constant annual problem of not knowing what to buy that certain individual for Christmas? You just can never find that unique gift that will totally surprise and enthrall the recipient? Well I thought that I would prepare a list of some of the more unusual gifts that I have given to my loved ones on Christmas morning, in hope that it may be of use to others.

How about an "Osama Bin Laden Doll"? This bearded, dark-skinned doll sits in a permanent cross-legged position. The main feature of this doll is that you can never find it. This feature is great for parents because you will never find it lying around the house constantly underfoot. Another bonus is that you never have to look at it. It also comes with seven interchangeable turbans, one for each day of the week.

For that little nephew who has everything, Mattel has an interesting new toy simply called "The Gas Powered Sharp Thing". Fifteen rows of precisionally sharpened blades rotate at high speed on a drum that is powered by propane fuel. It can be used as a paper/cat shredder, a catapult when filled with rocks, a dissector, blender, and can also be used along with your Osama Bin Laden Doll, if you can find it. This toy is guaranteed to unglue any nephew from his computer and will probably keep him away from it for some time as he recovers in hospital.

How about for that Uncle of yours who insists on giving you useless gifts that are totally impractical and ugly? How about an inflammable tie for 'good ol' Unc'? This seemingly normal necktie bursts into flames upon coming in contact with turkey gravy. This gift also serves as a great highlight to the family festive Christmas dinner. You can just feel the excitement mount as you hear your Uncle's request from the other end of the table; "Can someone please pass me the gravy?"

And then there is the ever-popular chemistry set for boys, and the cooking set for girls. These sets come with all kinds of white powders that will drive parents crazy! They'll never figure out what you're tampering with. Also included are various fire producing apparatuses such as Bunsen burners, gas powered stoves, hot plates, charcoal, matches, and napalm ingredients.

For the person who likes to travel	– a bus pass.
For the person who has everything	- get them nothing.
For the lover of country music	-CD of Boxcar

Willie's biggest hit (he only had one) "My train is off it's track since you left me standing at the alter in my skivies".

For that relative that drives you crazy

- a gift certificate for five sessions with a Psychiatrist (this gift is tax deductible)

For the husband

- a city road map disguised as a newspaper so that he doesn't have to be concerned with anyone seeing him using it.

For the wife

- a $2,000 gift certificate for La Vie En Rose

For the lover of classical music

- the complete 'Handel's Messiah' harmonica solo performed by Cedric Phlim.

For the TV series
fanatic
    - VHS box set of the
complete Gomer
Pile Series

For the party
animal
    - a gift certificate
for the Hutterite Gift
and Party Shoppe
just outside of town

For that red-neck
cousin
    - "Hee Haw, the
Movie I"

For the avid golfer
    - the book "The
Importance of the
Father in the Home"

For the more
senior loved one
    - a CD by Tiny Tim
and Tennessee
Ernie Ford entitled
"Tip Toe Through
the Coal mines."

For the backyard
mechanic
    - a backyard that is
far away from
where **you** live.

For that 'boring guy'
    - black socks and a
black thong

bathing suit(which will most probably be worn as a combo)

For the 'couch potato'

- a mini fridge that comes on wheels with a belt that can be tied around the waist which will then allow the fridge to follow the potato wherever he/she may go.

For the parents who don't need anything

-something that **you** need

For that ex-friend

- the book "How to be Popular, Even When You're Ugly"

I sincerely hope that some of these suggestions help you in your annual Christmas shopping outings.

Christmas List 2

Hey kids! There's a new toy that has recently come out that you will just love to own. So begin pestering your parents for it **now**. Don't wait for the Christmas rush! Let them know in plenty of time that you just **have** to have this toy or that there will be consequences.

This brand new incredible toy invention is "<u>Frosty the Throwman</u>".

This plastic snowman stands four feet tall and has a motorized arm that can fire snowballs at various speeds. It operates on the same principle as a baseball-pitching machine. The velocity of the snowball may be varied between twenty-five to one hundred miles per hour.

This little snowman is great for those friendly neighbourhood snowball fights, or for those annoying neighbourhood cats, or for target practice using your unsuspecting little brother as the target to practice on.

Frosty's range is approximately one hundred yards, so you don't have to ever worry about getting caught. He is also very light and portable which comes in handy when you have to vacate an area very quickly.

Of course Frosty can also be converted in the summertime to huck rocks, tomatoes, or heads of lettuce. Mom can even conscript Frosty when the occasion arises to propel household objects at your Dad when he mis-behaves.

If your parents are thinking about building a new garage, be quick to point out that if they enclose Frosty in the old garage with plenty of ammo, and set his dial to the one hundred miles per hour 'lightning' setting, he will totally demolish the old garage in less than fifteen minutes.

Look for "Frosty the Throwman" in most stores this Christmas. He only costs seventy-five dollars. If you happen to have a brother or sister, hit your parents up for a Frosty for each of you stating that it would be unfair to have snowball fights without at least one Frosty per side.

"Frosty the Throwman", makes a great gift!

And here are some more great gift ideas for the whole family:

For teenagers   - a brand new festive CD by the group "The Defiant Pumpkins" contain-ing a mixture of traditional and orig-inal Christmas music.

For the follically
challenged man
(men) in your life

Books on baldness:
"Toupee or not
Toupee"
"Hair Apparent"
"Help in Grieving for
a Lost Friend"
"Hair Today,
Chrome Tomorrow"
"How to Steam
CleanYour Rug"

For the person who loves to cook and is not intimidated by all of that "health food crap", there is a new book just out on the market by "The Hobbling Gourmet" entitled"Cooking With Cholesterol". (His case of gout has almost cleared up)

For that annoying
friend

- the book, "Life, for
Dummies"

For that annoying
parent

- a gift certificate for
two body piercings

New Trends   - snowshoe football
                                No holds barred
                                checkers

For the extremely   -glow bowling gift
desperate shopper   certificate
                                -a set of spark plugs
                                -velvet picture of
                                Elvis

Be sure to carry this practical list with you at all times during the Christmas shopping season.

Uncomfortosis

"Dear Counselor,

I am suffering from a very common, but excruciating disorder that I've noticed is not exclusive to myself. I know that you usually deal with "romantic" relationships, but I didn't know where else to turn.

I suffer from a disorder called "uncomfortosis", commonly referred to as 'the uncomfortable feeling that one experiences when traveling in an elevator with one or more complete strangers".

I am in dire need of some serious help.

As I stepped into the elevator this morning, I was *greeted* by six other individuals whom I had never seen before in my entire life. I say *'greeted'* in it italics, because they really only glanced up to make sure that I wasn't carrying any weapons, and then they resumed their previous statuary positions staring at the floor.

Everything was quite comfortable until the door closed. That's when the effects of this horrid disease took over.

Symptoms included everything from an uncontrollable urge to examine the other passenger's feet, to a magnetism-like force draw-ing my eyes to the little numbers above the door. I've learned to manage these prob-lems... but the silence!!! **I can't stand the silence!** Sure, every once in a while someone would clear their throat, or cough, and every-one would then raise their eyes slightly to see who made the noise, but mostly, it is just quiet. **The silence is deafening!** It scares me! Is there anything that I can do?

"Jim", from the 8th floor"

Dear "Jim",

Actually Jim, there are many 'romantic' relationships that take place in elevators, so I feel quite comfortable addressing your prob-lem. You are one hundred percent correct in stating that this is a very common affliction.

I will attempt to answer your question in two parts. The first will deal with the elevators that you ride at work, i.e. everyday, day in and day out, where you would often ride with the same people several times over the course of a year. The second part will deal with elevators that are elsewhere, that you would ride infrequently, where the passengers would be total strangers. This would be in such locations as department stores, or apartment blocks and office buildings other than where you live and work.

First, at your office building. I could just *feel* your anxiety leap right off my computer screen as I read your letter on my e-mail. If you have no intention of <u>ever</u> speaking with any of these Bozos, then just frown and scowl at each and every one of them who tries to make eye contact with you as you enter the elevator. This will stop them from trying to get friendly with you, and it will also keep your face in good shape. (Please see "<u>I Love to Frown</u>" included in this book somewhere)

Always carry a Walkman with you and wear the headset. Whether or not you actually have the thing turned on, or whether you even have batteries in it, is inconsequential. Most passengers won't speak to you because they will think that you can't hear them. If they are spiteful enough to speak to you anyway, you can just ignore them by *pretending* that you can't hear them. If you choose to turn the Walkman on, this will also solve the silence problem for you. If you close your eyes and sway to the music, a la Stevie Wonder, you won't have to stare at the lighted numbers or the other passengers' feet. Once in a while you can sing along with the music. This practice usually <u>assures</u> you that no one will ever speak to you in that building, let alone in the elevator, ever again.

Now, any other elevator. If you don't have your Walkman with you, and you can't stand the silence, and you are with strangers, you can just start up a quick conversation without even looking at them. Just very nonchalantly utter something like, "Did you know that more people die in elevators every year than in airplanes?" or, "Is that smoke I'm smelling?" or while pretending to read the operating license on the elevator wall, "Gee, this elevator was last serviced in 1938. Imagine that!"Any of these little quips should solve the silence problem. And the great thing about them is that you can use them over and over again, because you always use them with strangers whom you most likely will never see again in your lifetime!

If any of the passengers happens to stay clear-headed and utters the phrase, "Public mischief", immediately exit the elevator at the nearest floor.

I hope that these suggestions help you with your problem, Jim, and if they don't, there's always the stairs!

The Counselor

Etiquette, Schmediquette

"Dear Counselor,

I have a very embarrassing problem that has been hounding me for years. I am hoping that you will be able to help me with your advice.

Whenever I am at a party of any kind where food and drinks are served, or if my date takes me out for dinner, I get extremely paranoid.

My problem, is that while I am eating and socializing, I quite often will spit food at the person I am in conversation with. Sometimes they notice this and sometimes they don't. I never know how to react, what to do or say.

I have visited my dentist to see if my teeth are the problem, but he assured me that my teeth were not at the root of my problem.

I **can't** stop going to parties or on dates with guys, but I also seem not to be able to stop spitting food at people that I am talking to.

Can you help me at all?

Emma"

Dear Emma,

Thank you for sending me your letter. Did you happen to read the letter aloud to yourself while eating an apple just before mailing it to me? Just wondering.

Everybody will from time to time experience this embarrassing situation. This is the first time that I have encountered a **chronic case** of "food spitting" however.

I will list a number of possible solutions that will deal with this problem, as it may occur in a variety of situations. I hope that one or more of them will be of use to you.

In most situations it is best to always make light of the faux pas. If you find yourself seated at the family dinner table at Thanksgiving or at Christmas with parents and other loved ones, and you accidentally spit a piece of turkey back onto the serving platter, or you extinguish one of the candles with a mashed potato missile, boisterously, so everyone can hear you, brag what an accurate shot you are. This will inevitably bring about roars of laughter and the moment will pass along quickly without another word being said about it.

If you are attending a party at which all of the people,(or at least the person that you are spitting at), are friends, again make light of the situation by saying, "That piece of shrimp stuck to your blouse really coordinates nicely with the jacket you're wearing", while at the same time flicking the morsel of food off of the recipient with your thumb and index finger.

If this same situation presents itself but you are speaking to a stranger, very quickly wipe the wayward food from his or her clothing with a napkin saying at the same time, "My mother always taught me to share."

If on the other hand you are in a heated debate or argument with someone that you don't particularly care for, and you find yourself peppering your victim with a buffet of finger food bits, an apology is **not** necessary, but you still should wipe down the front of his or her attire while saying,"And another thing, those are **my** hors d'oeuvres! Go get your own!"

At formal receptions, when conversing with another woman who is wearing an evening gown, and you nail her on the chest with an errant escargot, just compliment her on her beautiful and unusual brooch and then wave to no one in particular on the other side of the room calling out, "Hello Pete", and then excuse yourself to go and talk with him.

If speaking to a woman who happens to be considerably shorter than you are, and the tidbits of food are sticking in her hair like mosquitoes in a bug zapper, don't do or say anything. She'll never know.

The most difficult situation to be in of course, is when your food flicking follies begin when you are with someone that you genuinely wish to impress. If your date takes you to a fine restaurant for dinner, and you find that your extreme nervousness coupled with your Beef Wellington is causing you to mimic a Gatling gun, I would suggest that you come clean, so to speak. Tell him the truth. You do not want to begin a prospective relationship under any hood of deceit. It would be much better for all concerned if he knew right up front that if the relationship is to continue, that he will be acting as a backstop for your frequent, delinquent spitballs.

If, however, you decide to go with the alternative choice, i.e., lying, then you must always be prepared to be thinking ahead in order to camouflage your menacing mastication. For example, when in a restaurant, always insist on sitting **beside** your date and **not across** from him. If he should question this, just tell him that you want to be close to him at all times. If this ploy simply cannot work, always carry a veil in your purse and hang it from each of your ears to cover your mouth just as the food arrives at your table. You can explain that this is a religious custom that you strongly believe in, or that you like to play a game called "The Way of the Romans" occasionally. Remember however, that this will oftentimes leave you open to peeling grapes for your date later on in the evening when he invites you back to his apartment to show you his toga.

I sincerely hope that some of these suggestions will be beneficial to you. Write me again sometime to let me know how things are going. Please write after you have completed your dinner.

Yours truly,
The Counselor

TO ORDER THIS BOOK PLEASE CONTACT:

PRAIRIE WIND BOOKS
83 BRIGHT OAKS BAY
WINNIPEG, MB.
R2M 2L9

PHONE: (204) 253-7729
FAX: (204) 669-0947
E-MAIL: prairiewindbooks@hotmail.com

Printed in the United States
1402800001B/67-84